I Am N

"There is no doubt that radical Islam is one of the greatest challenges facing the church today. These inspiring accounts of the persecuted church will move you to tears and then drive you to your knees. We all have a scriptural responsibility to stand up for and stand with our brothers and sisters who are going through the fire. Don't let the horrors described here intimidate you, because fear is a terrorist's greatest weapon. Instead, be stirred up to pray that the Holy Spirit may give you boldness to speak out, to take action, to get involved. Similarly, don't let these indescribable crimes fill you with hate for Muslims. Many Muslims would join us in condemning these atrocities. We are called to follow our Savior in loving our enemies, serving their needs, and having compassion on their blindness. The sacrificial faith of the suffering saints described in this book show us all how we are to respond at this time of crisis, courageously daring to love Muslims with the love of Christ."

Julyan Lidstone
Operation Mobilization (OM)

"VOM's *I Am N* is a challenging mosaic of stories that remind us of normal Christianity, faith that is lived out in persecution. There are a lot of reminders within the pages of this book. We are reminded that there are no such entities as a 'free church' or a 'persecuted church'; there is simply *one church*, always persecuted and free. The church in persecution teaches us how to pray, not that their persecution might end but that they might be obedient through their sufferings. This is a prayer that prays both halves of the prayer of Jesus. It is always appropriate to pray for 'let this cup pass' while never forgetting to pray to the Father that 'thy will be done.'"

Nik Ripken
International Mission Board (IMB) of
the Southern Baptist Convention
Author of *The Insanity of God* and *The Insanity of Obedience*

"Islamic terrorism is often the lead news story of the day, but Jesus promised to build his church and that the gates of hell would not prevail against it. So although terrorism grabs the headlines, Jesus's followers are flourishing right in the heart of the danger. *I Am N* was written to tell the stories of brave believers on the front lines of today's raging spiritual battle. Their courage will inspire you to think differently, live differently, and your heart will be refreshed as you get to know them. I believe they have become the new face of Christianity and we can learn much from them. The word *retreat* is foreign to the gospel. Brothers and sisters who live in harm's way today are in no way waving white flags. Instead, they're yelling 'Charge' and taking the gospel to the ends of the earth even if it costs them their lives."

Tom Doyle
e3 Partners
Author of *Killing Christians: Living the Faith Where It's Not Safe to Believe*

"Instability is our new normal. The gospel must ever be preached under pressure, and we must give up the idea that we can truly stand up for Jesus anywhere in the world without suffering for him. The only people in the world who can avoid the equal and opposite errors of Islamophobia and naive accommodation are the followers of Jesus who love Jesus enough to share in his sufferings and who love Muslims enough to suffer and die for them."

Dick Brogden
Assemblies of God World Missions
Author of *Live Dead Joy: 365 Days of
Living and Dying with Jesus*

"The further we are removed from the suffering of others, the easier it is to do nothing. We must not allow ourselves that option. Through these stories, please allow yourself to draw near to our persecuted brothers and sisters. In my role as a leader of a missions agency reaching out to Muslim people, I've been pulled into the suffering. Personal friends have been beaten, imprisoned, tortured, or killed. My tears, sleepless nights, and prayers didn't seem enough. I am extremely grateful for a partnership we now have with The Voice of the Martyrs. In practical ways they are helping us deal with the persecution and showing us how to get back up and press on with the good news of God's love through Jesus. This book will help us all respond in compassion."

Kevin
Missions executive with more than thirty years of service in restricted and least-reached nations

"It has been our honor and privilege to pray, weep, and serve alongside brothers and sisters who have suffered for Christ at the hands of their families, neighbors, and governments. As we recall their faces and tell their stories, we join the apostle Paul in saying, 'I thank my God every time I remember you … I always pray with joy because of your partnership in the gospel from the first day until now' (Philippians 1:3–5). God is at work in extraordinary ways in the midst of the worst possible terror, oppression, and violence. The Christians you will meet in this book reveal a hope and strength that is both supernatural and eternal. These family members have completely abandoned their personal agendas and are learning to trust God absolutely. We have much to learn from their example."

Cole, Cheryl, and Jason
The Voice of the Martyrs
Executive editors, *I Am N*

i am n
devotional

the voice of the martyrs

i am n
devotional

David C Cook

transforming lives together

I AM N DEVOTIONAL
Published by David C Cook
4050 Lee Vance View
Colorado Springs, CO 80918 U.S.A.

David C Cook Distribution Canada
55 Woodslee Avenue, Paris, Ontario, Canada N3L 3E5

David C Cook U.K., Kingsway Communications
Eastbourne, East Sussex BN23 6NT, England

The graphic circle C logo is a registered trademark of David C Cook.

The website addresses recommended throughout this book are offered as a
resource to you. These websites are not intended in any way to be or imply an
endorsement on the part of David C Cook, nor do we vouch for their content.

Details in some stories have been changed to protect
the identities of the persons involved.

All Scripture quotations are taken from the ESV® Bible (The Holy Bible,
English Standard Version®), copyright © 2001 by Crossway, a publishing
ministry of Good News Publishers. Used by permission. All rights reserved.

LCCN 2015956444
ISBN 978-0-7814-1401-2
eISBN 978-0-7814-1411-1

Manuscript written by Judy Gordon Morrow

Printed in the United States of America
First Edition 2016

1 2 3 4 5 6 7 8 9 10

121815

Day 1

As they were going along the road, someone said to him,
"I will follow you wherever you go." And Jesus said to
him, "Foxes have holes, and birds of the air have nests,
but the Son of Man has nowhere to lay his head."

Luke 9:57–58

Searching "Home, sweet home" garnered 297 million results on Google, which shouldn't surprise us. *Home* is a cherished word—a word that tugs at our heartstrings. We hold in honor that place of refuge where we can relax and be real.

Our lives revolve around our homes, whether that entails a new project, a gathering of friends and family, or simple daily routines. We arise to our beverage of choice and retire with a favorite pillow. Every little thing we need and use is there: bath towels, pans and dishes, shoes and clothing. Our personal and valued stuff—from treasured mementos to the latest gadgets—contributes to our sense of home.

Entwined in the practical elements of where we live is that indefinable essence of home, that familiar place where we belong. Haven't we all said, "I just want to go home"? No wonder the words "Welcome home" so resonate within us.

Now put yourself in the place of Abu Fadi and his wife of Iraq, whose lives were disrupted with the news that ISIS had moved into their hometown. They, along with thousands of others, escaped with nothing and ended up in a refugee camp. Forced to abandon their home, they also lost the rhythm of life that defined their days.

Place that template over your residence and routine, and imagine going from your home of plenty to a tarp lean-to where even food and water are scarce. Envision yourself surrounded by others suffering the same plight, with everyone longing for homes left behind. Abu and his wife forfeited their beloved home and future plans, all because they would not denounce Jesus.

Going Deeper

When you hear the word *home*, what emotions does it evoke? Now juxtapose the image of a tarp lean-to in a refugee camp with a picture of the place you call home. How does that contrast make you feel? Perhaps sketch that scene and place it in your Bible to remind you to pray for the countless displaced Christians in our world today.

Lord Jesus, as we slip into our cozy beds tonight and pull up blankets to keep us warm, bring to mind our brothers and sisters who had to flee their homes and have lost all things comfortable and familiar. Although we realize that material things aren't of utmost importance in light of eternity, we confess that we like our creature comforts and enjoy our way of life.

Abu and his wife gave thanks to you in the refugee camp. Help us duplicate their hearts of gratitude no matter what situation may disarm us. And remind us to pray for them and the thousands of others who have been ripped from their homes because of their loyalty to you. May we hold loosely what you have given us, so that we can live largely for you and your coming kingdom. Amen.

Day 2

The Spirit himself bears witness with our
spirit that we are children of God.

Romans 8:16

What is your identity? What defines you? If your friends were to place one label on you, what would it be? Of course we all assume multiple identities as varied as our roles in life. But for now, strip away all the roles, where you work or attend school, even where you live, and get down to the core, the very essence, of you.

When Abu and his family members were forced to leave their homes in ISIS-invaded cities of Iraq, it was because of one identity alone: Jesus Christ. ISIS soldiers, carrying spray paint in bags, tag the residences with the Arabic letter ن, or *n*, for Nazarene, identifying the occupants as followers of Jesus of Nazareth. With a red circle sprayed around the letter, it could easily be mistaken for a one-eyed smiley face.

But the grim truth has surfaced around the world, as many thousands have left their homes and livelihoods because of identifying with their Lord, Jesus Christ.

Identity is defined as the "character as to who a person is" and also as "the state or fact of being the same one as described."* So who are we? Will the real person match our description? Do we readily state with conviction that we are Christians, followers of Jesus Christ?

In our culture, standing firm for Christ doesn't result in torture or death, but it can have sobering consequences, as business owners and others will attest. Yet it is a matter of allegiance, isn't it? We have been so overwhelmingly loved by our Savior that we can't help but pledge our undying love to him. After all, no matter what our earthly consequences, what are they compared to our heavenly gains?

---

* Dictionary.com, s.v. "identity," http://dictionary.reference.com /browse/identity?s=t.

Going Deeper

You have probably seen the now infamous Arabic ن as the profile picture of Facebook friends showing their support for our persecuted brothers and sisters in Christ, choosing to "mark" themselves as followers of Christ and proclaiming to the world, "I am n." You might be one of those.

Try to imagine a world where the exterior of every home bears a symbol of the identity of the owners. What would your symbol be to identify you as a Christian? Perhaps draw it and place it in a prominent place as a way to profess your faith, your way to say, "I am n."

Lord Jesus, we admit that sometimes it is so easy to get caught up in the things of this world and the living of our lives that we don't know who we are anymore. We often feel like such a conglomeration of identities that we quickly forget who should be foremost in our thinking and in our living: you. In our heart of hearts, you are our highest desire, the one we revere above all, the Lord of our lives.

As we identify with you, Jesus of Nazareth, may the "n" of you on our lives shine with your love and forgiveness, your caring, your truth. We know that nothing and no one can compare to you, and we pray to be known as yours until that day when we see you face-to-face. Amen.

Day 3

But in your hearts honor Christ the Lord as holy, always being prepared to make a defense to anyone who asks you for a reason for the hope that is in you; yet do it with gentleness and respect.

1 Peter 3:15

We have often heard, and for good reason, "It's not what you say but how you say it." We could compile example after example of proof this is true. In fact, take a phrase—even "I love you"—and say it in every way imaginable, varying your tone and inflection and volume, and that will refresh for you the importance of how you say something.

But we never want to negate the importance of content, of course. What we speak and how we say it represent the God we profess. Abu kept both in mind as he was dealing with the interrogators in Iraq when he and his family members were leaving the area of Mosul that ISIS had invaded. Amid the intense stress of trying to get to safety, Abu prayed for courage.

God answered his prayer when Abu spoke his courageous answer to the guard's question of "Who are you?" at the first checkpoint. "We are Christians … not permitted to stay in this Muslim land." Refusing to let him pass, young men came loaded with firearms, asking more questions. Abu answered with honesty again: "We are Christians."

When pushed down to his knees to the words "Prepare to die," with an ISIS fighter wielding a sword above him, he prayed for strength and wisdom to be added to the courage he had already prayed for. When Abu was told it was his last chance to convert to Islam, God answered those prayers after what he thought would be a final glance at his wife, mother, and sister. "No, I do *not* denounce Jesus." The sword was raised, and he bowed his head, closed his eyes, and prayed—and God intervened.

The ISIS official who had just arrived decided to give Abu a message to deliver to his church leaders, declaring, "We are victorious. And we will follow you Christians all over the world. We will reach the Vatican and convert the pope to Islam if we have to."

Abu wasn't sure how to respond, but respect and honesty framed his answer: "We wish no harm on your people. Only to practice our faith as we please."

In return he was spit on and told, "Get out of here, you dogs."

At the next checkpoint, Abu again answered with honesty and respect during ninety more minutes of questioning. Again and again he was asked to convert to Islam. With polite firmness, Abu refused, saying, "I am a Christian."

Going Deeper

We have probably all cringed when hearing well-meaning Christians forget the crucial aspect of speaking God's truth in love. The message "God is love" is best heard when spoken with that very love. Envision dipping your words into the vat of God's love before letting them leave your lips.

Lord, when we see how in dire situations Abu answered those men, we can't help but think of you when you faced your accusers

and questioners just before your crucifixion. You showed honesty and respect, and it is clear that Abu learned from your example.

Thank you for this powerful reminder, Jesus. Thank you for showing us the humbling honor and beauty of speaking your truth in a loving and respectful manner. Help us not to be so intent on proclaiming the good news about you that we forget to do so prayerfully. We pray that our listeners will hear our love along with our words. Amen.

Day 4

I have said these things to you, that in me you may
have peace. In the world you will have tribulation.
But take heart; I have overcome the world.

John 16:33

The faith of Christians who endure persecution and torture for refusing to renounce Jesus can't help but inspire us. Yet most of us would confess that their stories also convict us. We wonder if we could withstand such harsh and unrelenting mistreatment.

Kazim of Pakistan spoke boldly for Jesus, which resulted in his capture and being forced to chop wood from sunrise to sunset. The ash-white handle of the ax turned to red from his bleeding hands. "Whenever I tried to rest, they beat me," he said. "This happened every night. They tried to force me to deny Christ, but I refused. The Spirit of God gave me power and guided me."

Eventually let go, Kazim was later apprehended. When a pistol was held to his head for several minutes, he stood firm for his Lord in the face of death. God intervened, and instead of the trigger being pulled, false charges of robbery landed him in jail, where he was beaten daily for two weeks. How amazing to read this in his story: "By now, the daily beatings had left Kazim weak, exhausted, and unable to speak. Pain radiated through his shoulders and across his back, and yet he felt a peace he could barely comprehend."

Did Kazim's tributes to God stop you in your tracks? Did you catch the acclaim he gave to his Lord in the midst of his misery? He declared the awareness of God's power and peace. Power to endure and peace in his pain. Yet that shouldn't surprise us, for we find solid promises of God's sustaining power and peace throughout Scripture.

Promises from our Father will prove sure—even in the perils of persecution—for all who follow and honor him. In fact, God's promises shine the brightest against the backdrop of despair. Hold on to God's promises and see how a single candle of faith can disperse the darkness.

Going Deeper

Do you wonder if you could stand firm in your faith and withstand whatever evil actions may be wielded against you? Jot down your fears, and then write out promises in God's Word to combat your every fear. Therefore, when your time comes to stand, God's power and peace won't fail you.

Thank you, Jesus, our overcomer, that you offer us the same power you possess. We praise you for the power of your Holy Spirit residing within us, always available and in abundant measure to match our needs.

We are so grateful for your peace, which defies all understanding and cushions us in our pain. Thank you for the example of your children, such as Kazim, who model your power and peace and encourage us with their unflinching trust in you. We pray for our fellow Christians around the world and praise you for their boldness no matter what the cost. Help us emulate their godly example of faith under fire. Amen.

Day 5

Convinced of this, I know that I will remain and continue
with you all, for your progress and joy in the faith.

Philippians 1:25

Our brother Kazim was finally let go and allowed to return home by the men who had held him hostage: the Muslims who had made him do backbreaking work and often beat his already broken-down body. If Kazim had then decided to stay home with his wife in the evenings, we wouldn't have blamed him. You know, keep a low profile, play it safe. Instead, he again chose to evangelize after his twelve-hour workdays as a farmer.

One night Kazim was accosted yet again by the same men at his home just as he was getting ready for his nightly routine. He pulled aside his young nephew, only seven, to give him his most precious possession: his Bible. Kazim's words convince us as to what he expected to happen. "Today they will kill me. Please take my Bible and keep it with you."

Shafiq, the stranger who appointed himself leader of Kazim's tormentors, was the one who held the pistol to Kazim's head for agonizing moments. He promised to shoot Kazim if he didn't declare Muhammad as the one and only true prophet. Looking Shafiq right in the eyes, Kazim refused. But he didn't leave it there. He told Shafiq, "If you want to shoot me, do it. I will happily accept being killed. But remember, if this is not God's will, you cannot kill me."

Going Deeper

Henry Martyn, a Bible translator and missionary to India and Persia, said, "I am immortal until God's work for me to do is done. The Lord reigns."*

Those words echo Kazim's statement, "But remember, if this is not God's will, you cannot kill me," and also ring true for Chuck, a former US Airborne Army Ranger. After some action-packed years of fulfilling dangerous army missions,

---

*   Henry Martyn quotes, AZ Quotes, www.azquotes.com/quote/662225.

Chuck turned to working as a stockbroker, running a gentleman's farm, and raising a family. Then a Christian publisher released his story as a ranger, and one thing led to another, including Chuck's traveling the world in pursuit of stories for a Christian television network. Many times this father of five has found himself in dangerous situations in oppressed countries, but he embraces the life God has given him and often quotes Martyn's words: "I am immortal until God's work for me to do is done."

How about you? Is fear holding you back from doing what God has called you to do? Surrender totally to God, seek his guidance, and see what doors he will open for you.

Lord, thank you for the courage and conviction we "hear" in Kazim's voice as he speaks bold truth in the face of convincing evidence meant to end his life. Thank you for his heart for you, which longs for others to know you so much that he is willing to put himself in harm's way.

We pray for Shafiq and the other men who endlessly tormented Kazim. We add them to our prayers for the thousands of Muslims who have made it their mission to torture and kill Christians. Father God, lift the blinders off their eyes and the darkness off their hearts, and shine in your light of transforming truth. Turn the blackness of night in their souls into the brilliance of new days found only in you, Lord. We pray for miracles of grace in the lives of these tormented men who torment others. Amen.

Day 6

And my God will supply every need of yours
according to his riches in glory in Christ Jesus.

Philippians 4:19

Shafiq's shaking hand didn't end up pulling the trigger, but he did make sure Kazim spent time in jail, suffering terrible mistreatment when he first arrived. Kazim was released on bail four months after his arrest, only to find his wife gone and Shafiq, his tormentor, in his home instead. Shafiq had claimed ownership of everything that had belonged to Kazim and his wife, Yasmeen, including their livestock.

Shafiq threatened to kill Kazim and his wife if he didn't leave immediately. Kazim found Yasmeen, and they fled the village and all that was theirs with only two dollars. Fear of being targeted caused more than one friend to turn them away when they sought a place to stay.

Yet Kazim's faith didn't waver. "I knew God would provide help, but I didn't know how he would help us." That *how* came from a Christian man in another village who provided a place to live, along with clothing, food, and a Bible. Other Christians came alongside and offered provisions, including a rickshaw for Kazim so he could support his family as a taxi driver.

In all the turmoil of that time, when he had been stripped of everything, Kazim reveled in this: "I had one blessing with me, and that was the freedom to preach the Word." He bears the scars of his beatings, but what is even more obvious is his joy in Jesus. "We forget all our worries, and even today we still feel fresh in Jesus's faith. I start each day in prayer and then drive my rickshaw."

Going Deeper

It is impossible not to love Kazim's heart that you hear when he says, "We forget all our worries, and even today we still feel fresh in Jesus's faith. I start each day in prayer and then drive my rickshaw." What is the "rickshaw" of your life, the daily work you do? Starting the day fresh in faith and prayer will help you "drive your rickshaw" with joy.

Lord, we are so inspired by Kazim and his infectious joy in you, his trust in you, his total satisfaction in you and your provision. Thank you for using this Pakistani man to be your messenger of love and truth to our hearts today. He endured so much at the hands of others as he was held hostage, tortured, and imprisoned, but no one could ever bind his spirit. He lost his every possession, only to find anew what he had already discovered: you are enough, and you will provide for our every need. Amen.

Day 7

All Scripture is breathed out by God and profitable
for teaching, for reproof, for correction, and for
training in righteousness, that the man of God may
be complete, equipped for every good work.

2 Timothy 3:16–17

Although the South may be known as the Bible Belt, America as a whole could be known as the Bible Country. No one can deny how we are abundantly blessed with copies of Bibles in our homes. Many of us enjoy comparing translations during our study of the Bible and own several. Now that the Bible is available online and with apps, the Word of God is literally at our fingertips.

Remember how Kazim made sure to give his beloved Bible to his seven-year-old nephew the day he felt doomed to die? He knew there was nothing more precious he could pass on to that child than the living Word. No better legacy he could leave than those pages of truth.

We know that Kazim survived and landed in jail, but God provided for his needs there with a worn Bible given to him by another prisoner. Holding that volume gave Kazim a sense of tremendous peace, but his swollen eyes caused by the beatings prevented him from reading it. He was thankful that his cellmate, who gave him the Bible, read it to him every day.

Just imagine how the audible Word of God gave light to that dark jail cell in Pakistan. Maybe there Kazim heard the words of the book of 2 Timothy, penned by the apostle Paul from a Roman prison cell. Throughout the centuries, from one cell to another, God's light continues to shine.

Going Deeper

The Bible read to Kazim in prison was in the language of Urdu, which has given us such words as *cushy* and *veranda*. Urdu is similar to Hindi, and the words are read from right to left on the page. The first complete Urdu Bible was published in 1843, although a New Testament was completed in 1745. You can find videos online to hear the Urdu language if you would like to get a sense of the words Kazim heard those days in prison.

When was the last time you read from the Bible out loud? When you can, substitute your silent reading of the Bible with enjoying it aloud, and hear the difference. Silent or aloud, Urdu or English, God's Word will shine hope and peace in a prison cell and in your personal darkness.

Lord, thank you for the Bible you provided to Kazim in prison during his four months there. And thank you for the ready availability of your Word to us every day in so many ways. Help us not to take it for granted, Jesus, but to treat it like the treasure it is. We pray to view your Word with fresh eyes and never forget what a gift it is for living in victory. Our prayerful desire is that our Bibles won't just take up space on the shelves of our homes but rather that your words of love and truth will take up residence in our hearts. Amen.

Day 8

Give thanks in all circumstances; for this is
the will of God in Christ Jesus for you.

1 Thessalonians 5:18

When was the last time you sat at your Sunday morning church service and wondered if you were going to make it out of there alive? That may not be the uppermost thought in the minds of believers worshipping in terrorist-infested countries, but it is the reality of their weekly attendance. Courage is a requirement.

Many of us heard the news of the horrific bombing of All Saints Church in Peshawar, Pakistan, that took place September 22, 2013, just as worshippers were leaving the Sunday service. The actions of two suicide bombers claimed more than 100 lives and left 150 people injured.

We hear those things and may even see footage on TV, but do we attempt to put faces to those numbers? Do we think about how the lives of our brothers and sisters in Christ have been profoundly changed forever?

Khalida is a woman willing to give us a face to that day of sudden chaos and destruction. Shrapnel ripped through her, killing her unborn child, due only a month later. Khalida herself sustained substantial injuries. And then the rods in her broken legs rusted, which further put her life at risk.

When she learned of the loving care of Christians who stepped in to help her by moving her to a better medical facility, Khalida's tears of suffering and frustration turned to tears of joy. She called her benefactors angels, along with all the people in America lifting her up in prayer. Instead of being filled with bitterness because of what happened to her, she was filled with thanksgiving for the help she received. Her gratitude compelled her to make church her first stop after her release from the hospital "to say thanks to God."

Going Deeper

Khalida prays daily with her mother, husband, and daughters after they read the Bible together. While they pray for Khalida's healing, the focus of their prayers isn't on only their needs. Even in the midst of heartache, they ask the Lord to bless the ones helping her. Think about others in your life who may be going through heartache. Lift up their specific needs to the Lord. Then consider Khalida and give thanks to God for his every provision and blessing in your life.

Dear Lord, we can't begin to grasp how much Khalida has suffered with the loss of her baby and then with wounds that almost led to her death. We thank you for the Christians who came to her aid, and we thank you for the example of Khalida's gratitude in the midst of such sadness and pain. We pray for her and the dozens of others who were wounded and for the families who will never see the faces of their loved ones again this side of heaven. What a high price this fellowship of

faithful believers has paid, and we pray that you will continue to comfort and strengthen them. Bring them to our minds when we attend the church of our choice this week, and instill in us grateful hearts inspired by Khalida. Amen.

Day 9

Do not think that I have come to bring peace to the earth. I have not come to bring peace, but a sword. For I have come to set a man against his father, and a daughter against her mother, and a daughter-in-law against her mother-in-law. And a person's enemies will be those of his own household.

Matthew 10:34–36

Have you ever been slighted by a family member? Perhaps you were deeply wounded by his or her words or behavior toward you. Yet, despite our differences, most of us are fortunate to know the support of our families. Within our family structure is where we feel safe; it is where we know we belong.

Imagine, then, being Nadia, an eleven-year-old girl in Pakistan. Once she learned of Jesus from her friend Rachel, who also gave her a Bible, Nadia's hungry heart opened to the truth and she accepted him as her Savior. She experienced grace in place of her constant efforts to keep rules and rituals. She was set free! But although she was free in her heart, she wasn't free to be open about her faith in her home.

Some people may be accustomed to the scenario of an older brother protecting his sister, but Nadia experienced the opposite. So offended was her brother, Miled, by Nadia's newfound faith in Christ that he beat her black and blue. He locked her in her room for three weeks, giving her minimal amounts of food and water.

The abuse continued even after she managed to leave home and eventually married a Christian man. He too was beaten by her angry brother. Because Nadia's parents filed kidnapping charges against her husband, the couple was forced to go into hiding.

Despite all the mistreatment at the hands of Nadia's family, she and her husband choose to serve God and trust him to provide for them. Christians came alongside them and helped her husband start a business that enables him to keep a low profile. They are thankful they survived the harsh beatings and continue to cling to God's promise never to leave or forsake them.

Going Deeper

The difference Jesus made in Nadia's life can't be denied. Her once-searching soul became so satisfied by our Lord that even regular beatings by her own brother did not dissuade her. Perhaps a family member has persecuted you in some way because of your faith. Take heart in Nadia's perseverance, and take a moment now to write a prayer for your family members opposed to believing in Jesus. Pray that the Holy Spirit would move on their hearts and turn their disdain into desire for our loving God.

Our dear Lord, when we see the sufferings of our brothers and sisters and the abuse they endure, we ask what you would have us do to help or what we can learn from their patient suffering. All around us, from next door to the other side of the world, are hurting people who do not have safe

homes in which to live and worship you. Help us to forgive those who have mistreated us and to reach out to those being mistreated because of their faith in you. Thank you for the testimonies of believers such as Nadia who stand firm in the face of great suffering for your sake. And thank you that you offer us that same strength and courage to endure the trials we are facing. Amen.

Day 10

And to know the love of Christ that surpasses knowledge,
that you may be filled with all the fullness of God.

Ephesians 3:19

Ali wrote in his prayer journal on a March morning in Iraq, "I am so full of the Holy Spirit that lives in my heart that my small body cannot contain the measure of the love he has given me." He didn't know that that day would be the last time he would see his family and that three days later he would die at the hands of terrorists.

Ali's body may have been small, but his heart loved others with a hugeness rarely seen. In the prior three months, Ali had won seven Muslims to Christ, yet he yearned to win so many more. He expressed his desire to his wife to win "one person for Christ a day, 365 days a year."

Ali knew his speaking of Jesus with others could be the very reason he would be silenced forever. He reminds us of Stephen, whose inspiring story is found in Acts 6–7. Stephen was one of seven men chosen to "serve tables" (6:2) so the disciples could devote themselves to prayer and the preaching of the Word. The requirements for those seven servers? "Men of good repute, full of the Spirit and of wisdom" (v. 3). Of the seven listed, Stephen is singled out with this tagline: "a man full of faith and of the Holy Spirit" (v. 5).

Did you notice the repetition of a word? "Full." Stephen more than fulfilled the requirement, because he was full of both faith and the Holy Spirit. But his "fullness" didn't stop there. Just three verses down we learn what Stephen was up to when he wasn't serving tables. "And Stephen, full of grace and power, was doing great wonders and signs among the people" (v. 8). Is it any wonder that when he was brought before his false accusers, "his face was like the face of an angel" (v. 15) and out of his "fullness" flowed a bold and powerful speech that led to his death by stoning?

Remember Peter and John when the Jewish leaders forbade them to speak any more about Jesus? How can we not be impressed by their response? "We cannot but speak of what we have seen and heard" (Acts 4:20). Their love for Jesus overflowed, and they simply couldn't help but speak of him, no matter the consequences. Ali and Stephen lived with that same passion for our Lord.

Going Deeper

We don't often think of "fullness" as a quality of a Christian, but it is God's perfect provision for the "emptiness" expressed by people before they come to know Jesus. Think of those in your life whose lives appear full but whose hearts are empty: family members, neighbors, coworkers, members of your local community, and beyond. What an exciting privilege that out of the fullness of God within us we can overflow his love to every empty heart around us.

Jesus, we stand in awe of you and your all-in followers such as Ali and Stephen, who both gave their lives to proclaim your love. Ah, and now we see what they had in common with you,

dear Lord—a love so deep that they gave their lives so others may know the life eternal found only in you. Comfort Ali's beloved family, and give them daily strength. Thank you for the fullness found in you—especially the fullness of your love—that compels us to share you with our neighbors and loved ones needing your love. Amen.

Day 11

For to me to live is Christ, and to die is gain.

Philippians 1:21

What gives Christians like Ali, a former Muslim, such a passion for Christ? Why can't they help but share Jesus with everyone they know? What fuels their desire for others to know our Lord when doing so could end their lives?

The only answer is love—the love Ali offered to others was born out of Christ's love for him. The love that carried Jesus to the cross changed Ali's life, and he became willing—joyfully willing—to risk his life for the eternal salvation of others. For him it was a no-brainer. How could he not share such great love and transforming truth?

Ali's life of love was framed and wrapped by God's Word. Each morning after his early arising, he would tack a handwritten Bible verse above the bed for his wife's awakening. Ali's time in Scripture was bathed in prayer—prayer that later in the day included his family, who also had chosen to follow Christ.

His prayers put words to his concerns for the hardened hearts of Iraq, but his love didn't stop there. He brought home the first man he had introduced to the "living water" and humbly and reverently washed his feet. This simple act of service flowed from his Christ-cleansed heart, an act of love he had learned at the foot of the cross.

Going Deeper

A man who professed to be a Christian once stated candidly that he didn't really love anyone beyond his immediate family. Maybe you know someone like that, or maybe that describes you. Yet how does that stance contrast with the command of Jesus to "love your neighbor as yourself" (Matt. 19:19)? Are you lacking in love for the lost? Spend time in stillness in Jesus's presence, in his Word and prayer, and recapture the wonder of your first love, Jesus. Replenish the well of your heart with his supernatural love, and be amazed by its natural overflow into the lives of others.

Lord Jesus, Ali's life so resembles yours, but we are keenly aware of our shortcomings when we look at our own lives. Take us back to the cross, dear Lord. Help us see again our sins for which you died and the suffering you endured. In light of your wondrous love, may we accept nothing less than to be flooded to overflowing with your love divine. We pray that out of that overflow, we would lead others to you with a joyful love that can't be suppressed. Amen.

Day 12

Set your minds on things that are above, not on things
that are on earth. For you have died, and your life is
hidden with Christ in God. When Christ who is your life
appears, then you also will appear with him in glory.

Colossians 3:2–4

Rebekah was married to Ali, the Iraqi man who loved his Muslim brothers so much that he died because of his passionate pursuit of their salvation. When he died, Rebekah lost not only her husband but also her best friend. Their three children—ages nine, seventeen, and nineteen—suffered the loss of their beloved father and also the one who led them to faith in Christ.

How would you react after such a heart-wrenching loss? Would you respond with anger toward God? Would you harbor a lingering bitterness toward your loved one? After all, if Ali hadn't been so set on "fishing for men" (see Matt. 4:19), in all likelihood he would still be alive.

But, no. We hear no resentment in Rebekah's voice, even though she also lost her home when Ali's Muslim parents kicked her and the children out after his death. Reduced to living in a one-bedroom apartment away from their church family, Rebekah and her children possess the "peace that passes all understanding" (see Phil. 4:7). In fact, reflecting on Ali's life and death, Rebekah offers words of wisdom. She encourages wives not to cling to their husbands but to free them for what God has called them to do—to "release them for ministry."

Is that easy for any spouse to do? Of course not. But despite her deep-felt grief, Rebekah views her life with "no regrets." Because of her suffering, she is stronger in her faith and sees life through the lens of eternity.

Going Deeper

When you review your life so far, can you say, like Rebekah, that you have no regrets? Do you wonder if that is even possible? It is true that much that happens in life is out of our control. Yet our response to those events, our attitude and perspective, does lie within us. When our hearts and minds—our very lives—are committed fully to Jesus, he gives us supernatural power to respond in godly ways. Out of our choice to follow Jesus alone will flow the indescribable peace of God. Do you need Jesus and his peace? Simply say a grateful yes to the Savior and entrust yourself to the one who loves you most.

Lord, we are prone to hold on to those things we consider ours: our spouses, children, homes, jobs—the list is endless. Yet everything we have finds its source in you, the giver of every perfect gift. Help us hold loosely everything entrusted to us by your hand. And help us see that everything tangible can never replace the intangibles you so freely offer: unspeakable joy, unsurpassed peace, the deepest love. Fix our eyes not on the things of this earth but on eternal things and when we will dwell with you forever in glory and unending joy. Amen.

Day 13

There is none holy like the LORD:
for there is none besides you;
there is no rock like our God.

1 Samuel 2:2

John's journey as a Christian began on his pilgrimage to Mecca as a Muslim.

One night in a dream while on his journey, John saw a man in white; his face shone when he spoke startling words to John. "My son, I see you are seeking after me, but the real faith is not in Mecca. I am not here."

When John arrived in Mecca, along with thousands of others, he walked around the Black Stone mounted on one of the corners of the Kaaba, a cubical structure housed in what is known as the Grand Mosque. It is toward the direction of the Kaaba that Muslims bow each day to pray.

God opened John's eyes to seeing his truth—to seeing light in the darkness. With sudden clarity, John saw the object of worship for what it was: a *rock*. That revelation dovetailed with the hypocrisy John had seen on his trip to Mecca, days that had been tarnished with moneymaking exploitations of the travelers. His expectation of holy footsteps had been trampled by the evil greed of people.

The turning point came when Jesus appeared again and answered John's request to tell him his name: "I am your God. I am Jesus Christ." Did you hear those words? They aren't just for John of Afghanistan. Jesus's words to John are for us all; they are for *you*. Don't rush by them. Jesus isn't just one god of many. No, he is the *true* God, and he is *your* God—the one who died for your sins out of a love so all-encompassing that nothing else in the history of humanity will ever match such a love.

John chose to believe Jesus—and later so did his wife, Mary—and although that decision raised his soul to heavenly heights, it leveled his life here on earth. Yet the love of Jesus lifts every sacrifice of a leveled life to a realm of pure and unsullied joy—a life of joy not tarnished by the ploys of humans but shining with the eternal purposes of God.

Going Deeper

Did you hear the disbelief in John's voice when he discerned by God's revealing truth that all the pilgrims were worshipping a *rock*? Yet God used that rock, the Black Stone, which has been reduced in size over the years, to lead John to himself, the Rock. Are you disillusioned and perhaps even crushed in your spirit by the "rocks" of your idols? Perhaps gather some stones to represent each idol of your life and then lay them down in repentance before the only one who deserves your worship. Then stand strong on the rock of your salvation and offer him your praise.

Lord, you are showing us even now our journeys to our personal Meccas, places that seem enthralling and enticing but leave us empty and dissatisfied. We might not have worshipped a rock, but we have worshipped idols with many faces: financial gain,

success, fame, our jobs, entertainment and recreation, our families, and even prestige within the body of Christ. Forgive us, dear God.

We desire to worship you, to embrace you with everything within us, so that we will be wholly yours and can live with the same passion as our persecuted brothers and sisters in Christ. We pray for them today wherever they are, and we pray you will ignite within us the same holy fire to worship and serve you with abandon. Amen.

Day 14

The LORD is a stronghold for the oppressed,
a stronghold in times of trouble.
And those who know your name put their trust in you,
for you, O LORD, have not forsaken those who seek you.

Psalm 9:9–10

As a devout Christian couple in Afghanistan, John and Mary suffered so much. John endured eighteen months in a bunker—a torture chamber run and overseen by his own father, a top Taliban leader. Usually used for anti-Taliban enemies, the bunker became John's residence where he survived the unleashing of dozens of snakes, followed by a vicious guard dog. John reported that God gave him power and assured him with the words "I am with you."

The calamities of John and Mary only increased with losses that Jesus himself gave forewarning of before John chose to believe in him. The seven things Jesus told John he would lose ranged from his parents and other relatives to his home and wealth. And then Jesus included the very worst loss for John and Mary: their dearly loved son, only two years of age. Yet knowing that, John chose to follow Jesus, and Mary made the same decision sometime later.

Any reader would be sobered by their story. How could this couple suffer so much and still remain steadfast in Jesus? When you intersect their lives with your own, you can't help but wonder how you would respond to the same treatment and devastating losses. You may have heard people use the expression "This isn't the life I signed up for," especially when they are going through a tough time. You may have said it yourself. Yet John and Mary knew exactly what hardships and horrible losses lay ahead, and they still chose to trust Jesus.

Why would they do that when they knew the horrific circumstances they would face? One explanation leaps out in their story: they had seen Jesus. They had been transformed by his grace and love. And once you experience Jesus, once you truly know his love, you are forever touched, forever changed. Nothing will ever be the same.

Going Deeper

The daunting difficulties that Jesus foretold to John stand in sharp contrast to the "health, wealth, and prosperity" gospel often touted in America. Can you imagine ending up homeless and losing everything, including your beloved toddler? But don't you also long to see and know Jesus in such a way that nothing on this earth can compare or compete with being fully committed to him? Seek the Lord—take time to truly seek him—and you will see and know him. And then, like John, you will want more people to see Jesus.

Oh, dear Lord, sometimes we long for those special visions and dreams of you, yet you have assured us in your Word that when we seek you, we will find you. Even if you choose not to come

to us in a visible way, you allow us to see you clearly by faith and through your Word. We can know you with a childlike trust that pleases you. We pray for John and Mary and the many like them who have lost so much. We lift them to you, grateful to have seen you, Jesus, the author and finisher of our faith. Amen.

Day 15

To grant to those who mourn in Zion—
to give them a beautiful headdress instead of ashes,
the oil of gladness instead of mourning,
the garment of praise instead of a faint spirit;
that they may be called oaks of righteousness,
the planting of the LORD, that he may be glorified.

Isaiah 61:3

Islamic extremism shows itself in a myriad of ways. Our hearts break when we read stories such as the one of John and Mary's son, only two, who was murdered and then, grief upon grief, photographed and brashly displayed on a Taliban website. The extremism continued with the murders by John's father of most of the other family members who professed Christ. And then Mary's father killed his wife with rat poison for her role in helping John and Mary leave Afghanistan.

Before they escaped Afghanistan, Mary was expecting their second child. Because she wouldn't bow to the wishes of her father to abort the baby or at least give him an Islamic name, her father beat Mary with punch after punch on her pregnant belly. That was after he slammed her to the floor and shattered her teeth. Then both fathers dragged her limp body to the bunker where her husband was held.

After their escape out of Afghanistan, John and Mary bore the brunt of more anguish: the doctor told them that the baby Mary was carrying was dead and that Mary would die too unless the fetus was removed. They had no money for the procedure, but they had God and prayer. Can you imagine the fervency of their prayers? And their joy when the shocked doctor told them on their return visit that their baby was alive? He declared, "How is this possible?" and pronounced it a miracle. That miracle led others in the doctor's office to Christ—more souls saved for eternity! Months later Mary gave birth to a healthy baby boy, God's gift of refreshing joy in the midst of a desert of sorrow.

Going Deeper

Our minds strain to understand such radicalism, such hate, such evil that John and Mary experienced from their own fathers. Yet God's light shone even in the midst of such darkness. A baby declared dead was brought back to life, and because of that miracle, others were born into God's kingdom.

Are you in need of a miracle? Are you tempted to think that miracles happen only to others or perhaps only to those in other countries? Take heart that our God is *almighty*, which means that he has absolute power over all things. Prayerfully bring to him your every need and concern. Like our brave brothers and sisters in Christ, you can trust our almighty God of unlimited power.

Our dear Lord, we are so apt to question and doubt you when things don't go our way. And then we hear of fellow believers such as John and Mary and shake our heads in wonderment at their steadfast faith. We pray that their example in the midst of

fiery trials will only fuel our desire to remain true to you. Thank you for every Christian in nations dominated by Islam. Help them stay strong in you. Provide for their every need. Help us walk with you in the same humility and trust, no matter how extreme our situations. Amen.

Day 16

The steadfast love of the LORD never ceases;
his mercies never come to an end;
they are new every morning;
great is your faithfulness.

Lamentations 3:22–23

In the midst of persecution is where the faithfulness of our loving God intersects with the faith of his obedient children. Shahnaz, a teen girl from Iran, found that out firsthand.

Her father, Ebi, was initially convinced that his daughter's interest in Jesus was a passing teenage fad, but Shahnaz boldly proclaimed that she wasn't just a follower of Jesus; she was a *passionate* follower of Jesus.

When Ebi commanded her to "leave this Jesus behind you," Shahnaz let him know why she couldn't with her simple response: "For the first time in my life, I am *content*!"

In his patriarchal role, Ebi was furious about Shahnaz's decision and worried about being humiliated in front of his friends. But unlike many other Muslim fathers, he said and did nothing, growing angrier and angrier. He knew that Shahnaz attended Bible studies and told her friends about Jesus, and yet his silence continued for two years.

When his daughter thwarted his scheme of an arranged marriage between her and a Muslim man and embarrassed him in front of the man's parents, Ebi's pent-up anger exploded. He yanked off his belt and whipped Shahnaz with both the belt and his words, demanding that she renounce Jesus and vowing he would whip her until she did.

Knocked to the floor by the belt, Shahnaz cried out, "Lord, I don't want to denounce my faith. Jesus, help me!"

And then a remarkable thing happened when the Lord answered the plea of his faith-filled child. Ebi saw Jesus with his arm around Shahnaz, telling him, "Stop beating her. She belongs to me." A miracle unfolded when Ebi took Shahnaz into his arms and asked for her forgiveness.

The miracle culminated weeks later when Ebi and his wife hosted a church meeting of Christians in their home.

Going Deeper

Just as he promised, God gives us new mercies every morning—mercies that sometimes take the form of amazing miracles of love, as in the case of Ebi. Recall times of God's faithfulness in your life when you saw his loving care in specific ways. That same God remains unchanged in his love and care toward you and your family. Is there someone for whom you have prayed for a long time, even many years? Don't be discouraged, but remember how our faithful God honors his faith-filled children. Truly, as with Ebi, he can transform hearts in an instant. Praise him for his coming answers of grace.

Lord, we can't help but marvel when we read accounts like this, where a hater of you and everything you stand for makes a complete turnaround in an instant. How can a devout

Muslim persecuting his daughter be suddenly transformed into a repentant father begging for forgiveness? Only you, God. Only you could so revolutionize a life by revealing yourself and your truth. Thank you for your faithfulness to Shahnaz as she grew in you and then stood for you with steady trust. Thank you that her parents also came to faith in you when that looked impossible. Continue to guide their family and all the Christians surrounded by Muslims. We pray that Shahnaz's example will shine forever. Amen.

Day 17

*The saying is trustworthy and deserving of full
acceptance, that Christ Jesus came into the world
to save sinners, of whom I am the foremost.*

1 Timothy 1:15

"It was easier to kill a person than a chicken." Do you not shudder when you read the chilling words of Alejandro, a Muslim terrorist in the Philippines? The only son of a strict Muslim family, he prided himself on his allegiance to Allah and believed his killings proved his worthiness and brought glory to Allah.

Can you think of someone in your life who is so deeply embedded in sin and evil that you think his or her chance of coming to Christ is impossible? Perhaps you can't even begin to picture that person as a believer in Jesus. Keep the face of that person in mind as we look at the life of Alejandro. This man who initially looked at his image in the mirror with pride for his evil deeds one day thereafter saw himself for what he was—a cold-blooded killer and terrorist. His pride turned to shame, and he left the militant group for a secular job.

Alejandro remained loyal to his Muslim faith, but then he met a Christian who invited him to church—not once or twice but until he agreed to attend. In that service Alejandro saw himself as he truly was: a sinner. But God gave him hope and let him know he could be a sinner saved by his grace. And then that hard-hearted murderer cried the first tears he had shed since his childhood.

Alejandro's story didn't end there. He attained his degree at a Bible school and went to minister in a remote area where Christians had been killed and the church abandoned. He traveled to neighboring villages on a water buffalo—a humbling change from his terrorist missions—to tell others the good news of Jesus.

And now envision this: Alejandro at a Bible conference grieving with another attendee over recently deceased relatives—a pastor, his wife, and children—killed by Muslim militants. What a beautiful example of the all-encompassing grace of God, which encircles all people and restores anyone who comes to him in repentance.

Going Deeper

Do you still see the face of the one you can't imagine as a follower of Christ? Prayerfully ask the Lord to allow you to see that same face shining with the love of Jesus, a person who has been redeemed and restored. If you are an artist, sketch before-and-after drawings of that person. Or use words in two columns to describe that person now and what he or she will be when rescued by Christ, as was Alejandro. Below the drawing or list, write a prayer of thanks, in faith, for what Jesus will do, and also pray to be used of the Lord to love that one to him.

Father, we are often inclined to write off certain people as being beyond your grace. We see in them all the clichés of being too far gone, too great a sinner, one whose heart is too hardened. We can

do the same thing with strangers whose dress and countenance cause us to jump to the same conclusions—that no way would they ever be interested in knowing you. Our vision is as faulty as Alejandro's was of himself, and both visions have one thing in common: pride. Forgive us, dear Lord, for thinking that anyone is ever beyond your matchless grace.

Thank you for the Christian man who invited Alejandro to church and persisted with his invitations. Open our hearts to those around us, and help us see them through your eyes—as souls bound for eternity and deeply loved by you. Fill us to overflowing with your love so that we can love others in the same way. Amen.

Day 18

Whoever denies me before men, I also will
deny before my Father who is in heaven.

Matthew 10:33

Ask people anywhere in the world what is most important to them, and a huge percentage will answer with one word: *family*. Family is linked with another endearing word, *home*, and most will do anything to ensure the well-being of their cherished loved ones.

Muslims who have accepted Christ and have become his followers are rejected by the ones they love and treasure most: their families. Think on that. They will know automatic rejection by their Islamic faith communities and beyond, but their support systems since birth—their families—will nearly always fall away as soon as words of faith in Jesus are spoken.

To be rejected and ignored by family would be hard enough, but too often the family's feelings of betrayal and shame lead to lethal acts. Despite that possibility, Suleiman of Nigeria answered his father's questions about his newfound faith in Christ with honesty and boldness.

His father's shock and dismay were compounded by the fact that in the past Suleiman had earned the reputation for humiliating Christians with his quick wit and intellect. And now this son had deserted his wealthy family's upbringing and traditions for the faith he had once despised.

When Suleiman wouldn't retract his belief in Jesus and later brought home his Christian wife, Elizabeth, his family's disapproval escalated. But Suleiman remained loyal to his Lord. "I'm not going to deny whom I serve. I'm ready to die because Christ is here."

Their lives threatened, he and his wife managed to get away, only to later have a mob descend on the building where they had rented a room—a mob hired by Suleiman's family and armed with automatic weapons. They escaped, and now ten years later their children have never seen their grandparents who disowned Suleiman and cut off all support to him and his wife. A family was lost because true faith was gained.

Going Deeper

In the years since he and Elizabeth escaped the threats of death from his family, Suleiman has often locked himself in a room to cry over the situation. But, as he explains, his tears flowed "because [his parents] were not going to heaven."

Most of us also have family members who don't know Jesus as their Savior. Do we cry over them and pray fervently and often for their salvation? How easy it is to get caught up in the daily affairs of life and forget that every life not committed to Christ is on a path to an eternal hell. When we pray for the Muslim families of our Christian brothers and sisters, let us also pray like never before for our families to know Jesus deeply.

Lord, for those of us blessed with the support of a loving family, we can scarcely put ourselves in the shoes of Suleiman and Elizabeth. We grieve to think that although Suleiman's parents are alive, they are missing out on being a part of their grandchildren's lives. We are sobered by the high price that

Muslims-turned-Christians pay, and we pray that you will strengthen them in their faith and reward them for their faithfulness to you.

We also pray for Suleiman's parents and his other relatives who so desperately need you, and we include the family members of all believers who do not share in the rich fellowship of Christ. And, Lord, we thank you anew for our families and the significant roles they play in our lives. Amen.

Day 19

By this all people will know that you are my
disciples, if you have love for one another.

John 13:35

A life of love is a life of sacrifice. Nowhere is that more clearly seen than in a refugee camp in Iraq, where in 2014 Christian volunteers worked long hours to provide necessities to the displaced men, women, and children. Azhar was one of the volunteers who faithfully stuffed and distributed Action Packs, plastic bags filled with food, clothing, and hygiene items. Tucked in each pack was also a Bible.

Azhar had met and befriended Ehsan, a Muslim who worked at an office job nearby, and they often discussed the Bible and Christianity. Ehsan questioned Azhar on many topics and even brought up Christians in northern Iraq who he claimed were hypocrites. Azhar prayed faithfully and answered his friend's questions with kindness, but Ehsan continued to shrug off anything to do with being a Christian.

When nearby Mosul was overrun by jihadists from the Islamic State, more Christians took refuge and additional supplies were needed. For two months Ehsan watched the tireless efforts of the volunteers. One day Azhar asked Ehsan if he would like to help. Ehsan agreed and worked a nine-hour day with the other volunteers, not even stopping for lunch.

Over dinner that evening, Ehsan started pelting Azhar with questions. "What kind of love do you have? What is the reason for this love?"

When Azhar pointed to God as the source of the love displayed that day, Ehsan asked for a Bible. Awake all night reading, Ehsan met Jesus, who awakened him to the truth in his Word. Ehsan believed and wanted to be baptized and get involved in ministry like Azhar. Love in action had opened the gate to truth.

Going Deeper

The refrain of a popular Christian song written in the late 1960s goes, "And they'll know we are Christians by our love."* The love displayed by Christians for the refugees, people they didn't even know, certainly led Ehsan to seek Jesus in his Word.

The first verse many of us learned as children was "God is love" (1 John 4:8)—only three words but rich in truth. Read aloud the familiar "love chapter" of the Bible, 1 Corinthians 13, and listen to it as if it were your first time to hear those words. Post a copy of that chapter in your favorite translation where you can see it often, and perhaps even memorize it. Meditate often on its words, and pray to love in that way—the way that will draw others to God and make a difference for all eternity.

---

*   Peter Scholtes, "They'll Know We Are Christians," F.E.I. Publications, 1966, www.hymnary.org.

Our loving Father, thank you for this profound and poignant reminder of how your love within us draws others to you. Help us remember that all the wisest words in the world won't win others for you the way love can. Your love given freely on the cross is so powerful and pure, and we pray to love others as you have loved us. No greater love can we ever know than yours, and we pray that we never take it for granted. Keep replenishing the wellspring of your love within us as we seek to serve others out of your ever-flowing, divine love. Amen.

Day 20

And your ears shall hear a word behind you,
saying, "This is the way, walk in it," when you
turn to the right or when you turn to the left.

Isaiah 30:21

God's ways are often different from ours, but, oh, the joy of following him! We can be grateful that a pastor in Bangladesh followed God's leading. Three times one Sunday morning he started to preach the sermon he had so carefully prepared for that week's special service, and each time God told him, "Don't preach this sermon. Instead, preach from the life of Joseph."

The pastor's faithful obedience is what kept Pintu Hossain, a seeking Muslim, from walking out that Sunday. He identified with Joseph's story, and after the service he and the pastor talked for two hours, resulting in Pintu accepting the gift of salvation through Jesus. Finally he found the contentment that had been lacking in his life as a Muslim.

God had orchestrated several earlier events in Pintu's life to converge at that moment. For years Pintu had been searching and asking questions, and his serious hobby of corresponding with pen pals from other countries took a new turn when he sent for a Bible correspondence course. He completed it in nine months, which led him to venture out to the church that Sunday morning.

Pintu's parents kicked him out of their home when they learned of his decision to follow Christ. But Pintu remained faithful and prayed fervently for his family, including his siblings who abandoned him. Can you imagine his joy when one by one he led those same siblings to Jesus? Now involved in radio ministry and a Bible correspondence course of his own, Pintu offers to others the hope he had been seeking all those years.

Going Deeper

Our lives are entwined with our fellow Christians around the world because of God's Spirit within each of us. Although we know only some of their stories, we know that we need to pray for them faithfully.

We all have our own stories of how Christ drew us to himself as well. Replay your story to yourself, or better yet, tell someone else the story of how the God of love pursued you. Recount his timely and loving orchestrations that have led you to where you are today. Perhaps you'll want to write out, or record via audio or video, the story of your salvation and subsequent walk with God to bless your friends and family.

Lord, we rejoice in your timely and loving orchestrations in Pintu's life. He is our brother in you, and we loved learning how you brought him to yourself. Thank you for the obedience of a dear pastor to give up his plan that Sunday morning for your higher plan. Bless and strengthen Pintu in his ministry as he brings your hope to many.

And, Lord, keep us ever aware of your still, small voice so that we won't miss your directives for our lives. May we be ever mindful that what might seem small to us you may choose to use in a huge way in the life of another. We long to walk in faithful obedience to you so that we won't miss any of your desires for us and others as we follow you. What a joy it is to partner with you for your kingdom! We praise you! Amen.

Day 21

Jesus wept.
John 11:35

The anguish so many persecuted Christians endure is beyond our ability to fully comprehend. Even when we try to put ourselves into those places of hardship, their trauma is too painful to even imagine. But try we must in order to enter into the abuse suffered by our family of God around the world, in order to "weep with those who weep" (Rom. 12:15).

The story of Mary of Nigeria is one we'd rather not hear because of the horrific details of the wickedness inflicted on her. Our pain only increases when we realize she represents hundreds of other young women who are being used and mistreated by members of Boko Haram.

Unlike fictional accounts we watch or read and can dismiss, these women cannot dismiss the unthinkable reality of being held hostage.

Mary witnessed the killing of her older sister, who had refused to follow orders to murder a man who wouldn't renounce his Christian faith. A friend, who was to have been married the day of their capture, was "married off" to a Boko Haram commander. Mary watched this friend's two sisters suffer the same fate. Mary herself was repeatedly raped, sometimes by five men at a time, one right after the other.

When her captors learned she was a Christian, she was forced to recite verses from the Quran and undergo other forms of brainwashing. Is it any wonder that she "forgot how to pray, how to read the Bible"? After being forced to lead an attack on her own church, she then learned she would be forced to marry the man who murdered her sister and had raped Mary many times.

That news propelled Mary and another woman to escape into the bush one night, and Mary made it back to her village, only to learn that her father had died of a heart attack after she and her sister were abducted. She is the only one left of her family. But she isn't alone. The body of Christ has come alongside her to help in her journey of healing, and God has promised never to leave her or forsake her.

Going Deeper

As ugly and evil as the men in this account appear, we need to remember that God loves them too. They are caught in a world of darkness that only God can conquer. Mary's sister was killed, and Mary's torture left her scarred; Mary suffered much loss in this life. But she possesses an eternal hope and future with Jesus. The men of Boko Haram have no idea what they have coming for eternity if they never see the light. Let's pray that God makes a way into their hearts and minds before it is too late.

Heavenly Father, words fail us to fully express our deep feelings of sadness and sorrow for what Mary has suffered. We weep for this young woman and the many like her who have been robbed of so much—their innocence, their youth, their tenderness of

spirit. Everything within us rises up in righteous anger at such atrocities and injustice.

Yet even when we might be tempted to rail at you and demand to know where you were when all that occurred, we already know the answer based on the truth of your Word: you were there. You were there even when your presence may not have been realized. You were there, because you have promised never to leave us or forsake us. We pray for Mary today and for all the other precious young women who have had much stolen from them. Restore, dear Father. Replace each layer of their pain with your supernatural healing, and renew their hearts with your perfect peace. Amen.

Day 22

We are afflicted in every way, but not crushed;
perplexed, but not driven to despair; persecuted, but
not forsaken; struck down, but not destroyed; always
carrying in the body the death of Jesus, so that the
life of Jesus may also be manifested in our bodies.

2 Corinthians 4:8–10

We have all heard the expression "Like father, like son," and never has a more moving example of that saying been given than in the case of Solomon and his father, Inoma, of Nigeria. Solomon had chosen to walk in the footsteps of his father's Christian faith even though more than half of their country professes Islam. Attacks by Boko Haram have increased in both frequency and intensity in recent years.

But it wasn't militant members of Boko Haram who turned on Solomon and his father on that fateful day in 2015; it was their Muslim neighbors. Men they knew and saw every day shot rifles and wielded machetes against them. The blow from the blade of a machete killed Solomon's father instantly.

The assailant with the machete red with the father's blood assured Solomon he wouldn't be hurt if he turned back to Islam. Without any hesitation, Solomon refused twice to deny Jesus. The result? Being doused with fuel and given another chance to turn from Christ. Again Solomon refused.

Today he wears the painful scars of the burns he received when he was knocked to the ground and a motorcycle ran atop his back. He couldn't escape the flames because of the weight of the cycle, and he'll never escape the pain from the skin grafts. Amazingly, he doesn't bemoan his disfigurement, but he does speak of his strengthened faith in Christ.

Solomon's words bear repeating: "I won't turn back. The salvation that I have in Christ was not free but paid with a price. Christ himself suffered to save me, so I feel I am prepared to suffer in persecution for the salvation I have in Christ."

Going Deeper

Solomon's words "I won't turn back" may remind you of the well-known song "I Have Decided to Follow Jesus." Each stanza ends with the repeating phrase "No turning back, no turning back." That kind of resoluteness is a rare commodity, and it hearkens back to the biblical heroes of Joshua and Caleb (see Num. 13:25–14:9), Esther (see Esther 4), and Daniel (see Dan. 6). Jesus is our greatest example, of course, and deserves our devotion to the point of death in light of his unwillingness to turn back from the cross. Let us pray to emulate his life and to echo his words to our Father: "Nevertheless, not my will, but yours, be done" (Luke 22:42).

Dear Lord, we are inspired and touched by how Solomon stayed true to the faith his father taught him—a transplanted faith that took such deep root it could stand against the strongest opposition. We pray for Solomon and for healing from the pain he deals with daily in his work as a carpenter. We also pray

for his attackers, knowing Solomon could see them again. He desires to say to them the very words you said on the cross, Lord: "Father, forgive them."

Thank you for the miracle that Solomon survived such a vicious attack. Comfort him and so many like him in their losses and pain, and give them your strength. Enable fathers and mothers all around the world to faithfully teach your truth to their children, both in your Word and by their example, so that their children will be able to stand for you as Solomon does. Amen.

Day 23

Blessed are you when others revile you and persecute you
and utter all kinds of evil against you falsely on my account.
Rejoice and be glad, for your reward is great in heaven,
for so they persecuted the prophets who were before you.
Matthew 5:11–12

Talking about Jesus with nonbelievers is rarely a safe subject. He came to be a stumbling block, and when we speak of him, reactions can range from derision to outright hostility. It isn't enough just to live like Christ in our homes, workplaces, and social settings. Eventually the time comes when we have to proclaim his name, even if that takes us out of the safe realm of innocuous topics.

Musa of North Africa remained in that safe realm until a coworker, also a friend, asked him a question one day. He wanted to know why Musa didn't take a break for the times of prayer at 1:00 and 4:00 p.m. Musa knew the moment of truth had arrived—the moment when he needed to speak the truth about his faith.

Have you noticed how the truth of Christ divides like nothing else? Every major religion of the world is graciously tolerated and often embraced—except Christianity. Although people welcome the concept that "all paths lead to God," they bristle with resistance to hear anyone declare that Jesus is "the way, and the truth, and the life" (John 14:6). That truth forces them to look up from the broad path of blindness that most choose and, instead, examine the narrow way of light that Jesus calls his followers to walk.

Musa chose anew the narrow way in that day of decision. He didn't want to hurt his friend, but he knew he needed to speak truth: "I am a follower of Christ." His honest words destroyed the friendship and led to his dismissal from his job following his friend's betrayal. But it only got worse, from deceivers who ambushed him to neighbors who demanded that he and his family leave their home or be thrown out.

Why did so many hard things happen to one man? Because he spoke truth. He chose to join the ranks of Christ followers and say, "I am in."

Going Deeper

Most people want to live in harmony with others, and that is an admirable trait except when it becomes an idol and we'd rather trade Christ-honoring convictions for the praise of people. Yet the truth doesn't change. The gift of Jesus's pardon never changes. He gave everything he had for you. Are you willing to do the same for him? Are you in?

Lord, when we think of the conversation Musa was engaged in with his friend that day, we can't help but wonder how we would have responded if we had been him. More than that, Jesus, we wonder how we would respond here in America, where, in most cases, we wouldn't fear losing our jobs and homes if we spoke truth. Jesus, help us not to value our own security and comfort and what people think of us above taking a stand

for you. Forgive us for times when we have been more bland than bold.

In light of the cross and all you suffered for us at Calvary, we weep at our desire to be well liked by others more than to be well pleasing to you. How shallow and soft we have become in a culture that has lulled us to sleep and lured us away from you, our first love. Wake us up, Lord! Remove the blinders from our eyes, open our ears, and help us see and hear your truth alone. And then unmute our mouths to unashamedly speak your truth with power and love. Amen.

Day 24

And he came to the disciples and found them sleeping. And he said to Peter, "So, could you not watch with me one hour? Watch and pray that you may not enter into temptation. The spirit indeed is willing, but the flesh is weak."

Matthew 26:40–41

What is your definition of prayer? Musa of North Africa began with his definition when he explained to his friend why he no longer participated in the prayer breaks at work with his Muslim coworkers. He shared his heartfelt conviction about prayer by saying, "Prayer is an intimate conversation with God, and it should be done all the time, in my heart, rather than at specific times using the same phrases and postures."

Here was a man whose life had been given to prayer to Allah—five times a day in a purposeful way—but through Christ he had discovered prayer to be so much more than a ritual, a mechanical act often done mindlessly out of habit. Since his conversion to Christ, he had come to view prayer for what it is: an intimate conversation with God. No longer a monologue, prayer for Musa became a dialogue with his divine Savior.

Today in America there is never a lack of interest regarding prayer. In fact, a search on Amazon for books on prayer yielded more than one hundred thousand titles. Impressive, yes? Christian publishers sometimes refer to prayer as an "evergreen" topic—one that always has a ready audience. And then there are television documentaries, magazine articles, and occasional news stories about prayer. But could there be more of a preoccupation with prayer than the actual act of praying? Are we ready to step away from the books about prayer and begin enjoying what Musa called "an intimate conversation with God"?

Going Deeper

Like so many others, are you tempted to "rate" your prayer life? You may rate it in a number of ways, from how often you pray to how long your prayers last. You may even give yourself extra points for remembering to pray for our persecuted brothers and sisters in Christ. Rather than focusing on the *how* of prayer, may Musa's story be a reminder to focus on the *who*. Prayer is not a list; it is a conversation and communion with the Lord. He simply desires to be with you—to hear your voice and know your heart. How about spending some time with him now? If it applies, you may want to start by saying, "I've missed you, Lord."

Oh, dear Lord, how the enemy of our souls tries to twist your truth about prayer. We pray that you will take away his veil of deceit and replace it with the truth of your Word. Thank you for the gift of prayer—for becoming the ultimate sacrifice for sin so we can go directly to you in worship and

gratitude and praise. What an amazing privilege it is to commune with you, our Creator and Savior.

Refresh or, if needed, reset our thinking in regard to prayer. We echo the request of your disciples, "Lord, teach us to pray." Open our hearts wide to receive from you what you wish to reveal to us. Unstop our ears so that we can hear your still, small voice. Help us pause this very moment to "be still" and in that stillness to know that you are God. Amen.

Day 25

O God, you are my God; earnestly I seek you;
my soul thirsts for you;
my flesh faints for you,
as in a dry and weary land where there is no water.

Psalm 63:1

If and when prayer occurs in our lives, too often it is done out of duty rather than delight. Perhaps it has become something to check off our daily to-do list so we can feel less guilty the next time we hear a sermon or podcast about prayer. It isn't that we don't want to pray—we do, and we know we should—but the busyness of life leaves little time to "be still." Together, let's look again at what our brother Musa has to say about prayer how is an intimate conversation with God.

We know what a conversation is, but what creates an *intimate* conversation with anyone? Wouldn't we agree that the basis for intimacy is a deep knowing of the person? Intimate conversation necessitates sessions of soul-to-soul communication that are rich and satisfying, where vulnerability and openness are requirements, and where the foundational and necessary factor is time spent in each other's presence. Time together is crucial.

We see the detrimental effects when we don't spend time with those we love, even if we had been very close at one time. Lack of time together leads to distance in the relationship. The same thing happens with God. Do you recall what Musa went on to say about prayer? "It should be done all the time, in my heart." *All the time.* The intimate conversation that begins with that set-apart, "be still" time upon awakening then continues all day long, between our loving Father and his grateful child.

Going Deeper

We long to be with those we love; we simply want to be with them. Do you desire that with God? Do you enjoy basking in his presence? A nonexistent or lackluster prayer life can stem from many roots, from unconfessed sin to disobedience. But often the deepest and most hidden root is a lack of love for our Lord, for whatever reason. No matter where your level of intimacy is with the Lord today, set aside some time to be with him, and then speak or write what's on your heart. Be honest with your words, and know that his arms are always outstretched to welcome you into his heart of deep love for you. Dwell there today.

Dear Lord, only you know where each of us is in relationship with you. You know those of us who revel in your presence daily and those of us who can't remember the last time we prayed. We are grateful that you love us all the same. Yet we know you desire fellowship with your children, and we see the difference it makes. We know if Musa hadn't been having those ongoing intimate conversations with you—if he didn't know you so well—how easy it would have been to answer his friend differently.

But Musa had gotten to know you, Lord. And in knowing you, he couldn't help but love and honor you. That is what we desire, Jesus: to commune with you all day long so that we will truly know you and fall forever in love with you. And may that deep intimacy with you always bring the strength to stand for you. Thank you, Lord, for hearing our hearts. We love and praise you. Amen.

Day 26

O LORD, you hear the desire of the afflicted;
you will strengthen their heart; you will incline your ear
to do justice to the fatherless and the oppressed,
so that man who is of the earth may strike terror no more.

Psalm 10:17–18

Remember when you were a teenager, the time of high hopes and dreams? You may even belong to that age group right now. Here in America, the teen years hold much promise and often culminate with a high school graduation and the right to vote. This is the age when expressions such as "You have your whole life in front of you" abound.

Ages ending with the word *teen* aren't the ones you would tend to correlate with slavery and repeated rapings, but that is the reality of many girls around the world. Hard as it is even to read those words, it is harder still to imagine such a life. In countries such as Pakistan, girls—even Christian girls—are employed by Muslim men to work in their households and are paid the equivalent of thirty-four US dollars per month. Financial constraints require young women to take these jobs and live in the homes where they work, but as it sometimes turns out, their employers are more interested in them than in their work.

Resisting their employers is often to no avail, and many girls also suffer physical and emotional torture. They are usually too ashamed to tell their families of the abusive treatment. And if they do speak up, it is not uncommon for an employer to make false accusations against his household help, such as stealing gold and jewelry, resulting in arrests and imprisonments.

Going Deeper

What can be said or done when we think of the savage acts of injustice perpetrated against innocent girls? Such despicable acts that cause lasting damage are beyond understanding. Rather than turn away in anger or frustration, we need to turn toward both the victims and the perpetrators with prayer. Prayer is the greatest weapon we can wield for those who are suffering and for those who don't yet know Christ. Then we can prayerfully follow up our petitions to God with any other support we can give as God leads. In doing so unto the least of these, we do it as unto Jesus.

Our Father, our hearts grieve over what is happening to these young women and that such things even occur in our world today. We are especially grieved when we learn of the overwhelming numbers of those who suffer this kind of abuse.

We bring these young women to you and pray that you would heal the wounds and scars of their pasts. Comfort their hearts. Give them hope and a future. We pray for the many who even now are being held in bondage where unthinkable acts are brought against them. Thank you for the Christians in those places who are helping and supporting these girls. Give us wisdom as to what we can do to help these dear ones, and then help us do it. Amen.

Day 27

And above all these put on love, which binds
everything together in perfect harmony. And let the
peace of Christ rule in your hearts, to which indeed
you were called in one body. And be thankful.

Colossians 3:14–15

Gulnaz is a young woman in Pakistan who has paid a high price. Married and a Christian, she refused a Muslim man's advances to the point that she slapped him. He carried through on his vow that she would pay for her disrespect and doused her with acid, leaving her with burns on her face, chest, and arms.

Such cruelty takes away our collective breath, does it not? This isn't a nameless, unknown person, but yet another young woman left with both emotional and physical scars, disfigured for life. Again God used his body when Christian medical personnel came forward to assist with caring for Gulnaz, even obtaining surgery to allow her more use of her damaged arm.

So what was Gulnaz's response to the acid attack? While her physical wounds healed, her spiritual life soared. God filled her with love to respond to the hate that generated the act toward her. Her story and witness touched the lives of young girls in her neighborhood, and a small Bible study was born.

But get ready for another collective breath—this time out of amazement. The run-down area where Gulnaz and her family lived had an open sewer in the street and garbage piled everywhere. Again Christians came alongside and made it possible for Gulnaz and her family to move to a house in a much nicer area. Yay, right? Yes, but for a different reason. Gulnaz and her husband turned over the house keys to a Pakistani evangelist who had been on the run ever since radical Muslims had targeted his ministry. After all, it was obvious to Gulnaz and her husband that the evangelist needed it more than they did.

Going Deeper

During prayer each week, a pastor invited the church family members to put their hands in front of them, palms down, indicating that they were giving everything over to God. Try it, with your fingers extended, and feel the emptiness and your inability to hold on to anything with your flattened palms. Picture God's hands under yours, receiving everything in your life, all given over to him. That is the way Gulnaz and her husband live, with no grasping but with giving all they have to our wise Father. Use that palms-down exercise when you find yourself wanting to hold too tightly to what was never yours to begin with. "Every good gift and every perfect gift is from above" (James 1:17).

Lord, how you convict and humble us with these true accounts of our brothers and sisters around the world. In our country we are so accustomed to certain standards of living that even

the poorest among us are better off than most of the world. We so easily forget that.

Here Gulnaz had been the victim of a terrible attack that changed her life forever, yet she responded with Christlikeness, determined that your love would prevail over the hate shown toward her. She even started a Bible study for young girls in her neighborhood.

Bless Gulnaz and her husband, and honor them for their godly example. Help us follow you in the same manner with hearts like theirs. Amen.

Day 28

When the righteous cry for help, the LORD hears
and delivers them out of all their troubles.

Psalm 34:17

Farid had just thanked God for his presence in his Bible study with five other men before introducing the book of Acts to them, not knowing the huge difference God's presence would make in the ensuing moments. Hard knocks at the door were followed by dark-clothed men with rifles and knives moving into the room. The scene of a Bible study shifted to this: Farid slammed to the floor, hands tied behind his back, a knife inches from his neck.

Miracle #1: In the chaos, clarity came to Farid to pray, "God, if this is the time for me to die, I forgive these people who want to kill me."

Miracle #2: Nothing happened! Farid followed God's leading to stand up, and the straps that had been binding his hands fell to the floor.

Miracle #3: He walked to the front door, where two armed men stood. One spoke chilling words: "Sit down, dog. You're not leaving—alive." The other pointed his rifle and pulled the trigger. Nothing. Twice the rifle jammed.

Miracle #4: In the diversion of the jammed rifle, Farid escaped, and the bullets that followed him missed him, hitting the wall beyond him.

Miracle #5: None of the other five men was injured at all.

What was discovered later proved to be the most chilling: a bag filled with evidence, including swords and a video camera, indicating the botched plan to behead all of them and produce a video to incite fear among Christians. But God intervened with miracle after miracle.

Going Deeper

All of us would have been crying out to God in that volatile and violent situation. But remember Farid's prayer? He told God that he forgave the men he expected to be his murderers. He explained later, "I wanted God to forgive them, and I wanted them to come to Christ as a result of my death." That attitude of love and forgiveness for his enemies is a miracle of God's grace.

What supernatural interventions of God's grace have occurred in your life? Designate a blank book or notebook as your "Miracle Journal" to record God's workings in your life. Then read for encouragement when you are in the midst of a needing a new miracle.

Our gracious God, thank you for your protection of Farid and his five friends who gathered that early morning to honor you. Continue to use their lives and witness for you, and help them be fearless in their walk with you. Use the events of that miraculous morning to inspire your followers all around the world as they recognize that you are the one who has numbered our days from the beginning. Thank you that until you call us home, you will provide for our every remaining day here on this earth.

We pray that knowledge will help all of us live in freedom, not fear. Amen.

Day 29

For thus said the Lord GOD, the Holy One of Israel,
"In returning and rest you shall be saved;
in quietness and in trust shall be your strength."

Isaiah 30:15

Sometimes as believers we can feel like the minority in America, even though our country was founded on the tenets of Christianity. But consider Malaysia. In 2011, at the time Jon's story took place, there were less than a thousand Christians in a country of twenty-eight million people. Put that into a percentage and you get this number: .0035714285714286. Imagine the kind of courage it takes to remain true to your faith in a country where Malay people are required to be Muslim and it is illegal to convert.

Jon exhibited that courage on a regular basis since his conversion to Christ six years earlier. He had become accustomed to the provocation by the police to report to them every three months; each time he politely refused to recite Islamic prayers and return to Islam, despite their insistence.

But when the police SUV showed up one evening after Bible study, this time was different. Fed up with Jon's resistance, three men forced him into the vehicle and blindfolded him for a four-hour drive. Surrounded by fifteen-foot walls topped with barbed wire, the "Islamic purification center" became Jon's torture center for the next three days.

Being bound, interrogated, beaten, kicked, and forced to sit on ice while naked were some of the methods of torment used against Jon. In everything, he refused to renounce Christ. Even this threat didn't deter him: "We are going to kill you if you don't confess the Muslim prayer."

Jon's response to those life-and-death words? He said nothing. They used a bamboo cane to beat him, demanding that he say the prayer, and still he said not a word. Instead, he told others later, he was immersed in a vision of Jesus himself being beaten. "I saw the blood of Jesus dripping, and then I heard the gentle voice of the Holy Spirit telling me not to deny Jesus no matter what."

Going Deeper

Although Jon had made some bold declarations during the three days he was tortured, the last session was filled with quiet drama and the power of God. When we read what he described, we sense we are on holy ground, reminiscent of the scene of Jesus with Pilate just before he was crucified: "But when he was accused by the chief priests and elders, he gave no answer. Then Pilate said to him, 'Do you not hear how many things they testify against you?' But he gave him no answer, not even to a single charge, so that the governor was greatly amazed" (Matt. 27:12–14).

Take some time away from all distractions and noise, and reflect on the power of silence, within your heart and as God's instrument in the lives of others. Look to the example of Jesus—and of Jon—and be prepared, if God leads, to say not one word.

Dear Lord, as we pray right now for Jon and our other perse-cuted brothers and sisters, we are grateful even to be considered in the same family. What they have endured and what many continue to face on a daily basis remind us of the grace and strength you promise to give us. Help us live so close to you that if our worlds were to be disrupted like Jon's—and our faith put on the line—that we would respond with the same confidence and assurance in you. Grant us the confidence daily that frees us to speak or be quiet, however you lead us, because the source of our strength is you. Amen.

Day 30

*[Pray] at all times in the Spirit, with all prayer
and supplication. To that end keep alert with all
perseverance, making supplication for all the saints.*

Ephesians 6:18

You have probably heard the expression "Prayer changes things." It may even be displayed on a wall in your home. The Bible is filled with prayers and scriptures about prayer that attest to the difference that prayer makes in a believer's life. The next time you see or hear "Prayer changes things," remember our brother Jon in Malaysia and the absolute truth behind those words. When he was picked up by the police and taken four hours north near the Thailand border to be tortured, Jon learned as never before the changing power of prayer.

When long-bearded Islamic scholars interrogated Jon for hours and urged him to chant with them, he refused. Later he relayed, "All I could hear was people praying for me." They poured buckets of water over his head, telling him he "must embrace Islam," and Jon replied with boldness, "I will not. Even if you chop my head off right now, it's okay. I have my God."

His boldness brought on beatings, and amazingly Jon didn't feel the pain or humiliation. Again he spoke of the prayers of God's people: "I believe the Lord came, and I could hear angels and the prayers of my Christian friends. When those men stepped on me and kicked me, that's when I felt the prayers; that's when I felt the presence of God."

Going Deeper

In what ways were you inspired when you learned how Jon heard the prayers of his friends during his three days of torture? Imagine how they prayed unceasingly for the deliverance of their brother. But beyond being inspired by Jon's story, how are you motivated to pray more? Although we can't say exactly how God will use our prayers, we do know he will hear them.

Heavenly Father, our hearts are moved to learn how you used the prayers of Jon's friends in such a powerful way while he was being tortured. Thank you for your mercy and grace toward Jon and for his steadfast faith in you. And thank you for his praying friends who diligently interceded for him.

We are in awe of you, dear Lord. Your ways never cease to astonish us, and we are forever grateful for your faithfulness to your children. We pray to recall the chorus of prayers that Jon heard when he was most in need of them as yet another reminder to pray for the body of Christ. Instill in us the will to pray so that our prayers will lift up brothers and sisters around the world and ultimately bring glory to you. Amen.

Day 31

The kingdom of heaven is like treasure hidden in a field,
which a man found and covered up. Then in his joy
he goes and sells all that he has and buys that field.

Matthew 13:44

Curiosity. A curiosity about people drew Abdul of Nigeria to become a witch doctor when he couldn't help but wonder what made them sick and what made them well. After five years in that role, it was that same curiosity that caused this Muslim man to wonder about Christians. *Who was their God? What do they believe? How are they different from us Muslims?*

Abdul started with the Quran, which he found had more references to Jesus ("Isa") than to Muhammad, the writer of the Quran. His research then led him to Christians, who understandably questioned his motives and feared for their lives. But Abdul wouldn't be deterred and showed up at a pastor's house at 4:00 a.m. to ask questions, which led to six weeks of sincere seeking and Abdul's coming to faith in Christ.

Rumors flew that he had been paid off to profess Christ; and to retain the family's honor, Abdul's brother determined to kill him for being an infidel. Instead, he too became a Christian, along with his three children. One is now enrolled in Bible school and plans to become a pastor.

Although at least three radical Muslim groups have tried to kill Abdul, who is now married with two children, he lives without fear. He echoes Paul the apostle and knows that "to live is Christ, and to die is gain" (Phil. 1:21). But his greatest desire is to continue to preach the gospel of Jesus so that more Muslims can hear the truth—the truth that includes what he tells every new believer: "You have come to suffer."

Going Deeper

It seems amazing that a man ensconced in witchcraft would turn his life over to Jesus. We can understand the pastor's reluctance to meet with him, can't we? Yet so often the people who appear to be the least likely ones to follow the Lord are in truth the ones desperate to make that life-changing decision. The lives they are living are devoid of purpose and joy, and the difference Jesus makes is distinct and transformational.

Think of an equivalent of the "witch doctor" in your sphere of influence. Your and his worldview and lifestyle may be polar opposites, but that person needs to know God's unconditional love. Pray often and fervently for the salvation of that one, show the love of Christ, and just see what God will do.

What a contrast, Lord, is our American Christianity to that of our brothers and sisters around the world. Abdul counsels your followers in the path of suffering, while we are often cajoled to follow a path of pleasure and prosperity. Yet you have clearly shown us who is richer. Thank you, Jesus, for shaking us from our shallowness and for opening our eyes to your truth.

We pray that you will protect and strengthen Abdul and his brother, their wives, and all their children. Raise them up as beacons of light in Nigeria, and use them to draw others to you, the light of the world. Thank you for their example of steadfastness in the face of constant uncertainty. Help us daily to support them—and all our extended Christian family around the world—with our prayers. Amen.

Day 32

*Therefore, since we are surrounded by so great a cloud
of witnesses, let us also lay aside every weight, and sin
which clings so closely, and let us run with endurance
the race that is set before us, looking to Jesus, the founder
and perfecter of our faith, who for the joy that was set
before him endured the cross, despising the shame, and
is seated at the right hand of the throne of God.*

Hebrews 12:1–2

Akhom and Hassani have names unfamiliar to us, but their
Egyptian hearts matched the hearts of many young men
here in America. Akhom at twenty-one described himself
as "away from the Lord." He said, "I was doing bad things,
living a life of sin."

Hassani agreed with his cousin. "God was not there in my life."

All that changed for the two young men the night a peaceful march of hundreds of protestors, including Egyptian Christians, erupted into chaos, beginning with rocks, bricks, and broken glass raining down on them from a six-floor apartment building. Confrontations began that escalated into acts of violence. Akhom and Hassani, though bystanders during the event, were drawn into the turmoil unwittingly.

A man shot Akhom three times in the face and once in the stomach. Another attacker took a machete to Hassani's face. Amazingly, they lived, but an even greater miracle occurred.

In the midst of healing from the vicious wounds they endured, the cousins have exulted in how that event revitalized their walk with God. From Akhom's mouth, with screws in his shattered jaw, come these amazing words: "The attack helped me to get closer to God."

His cousin Hassani concurs. "A new vision came after the attack. My heart was opened to realizing the grace of the Lord."

Going Deeper

We may be tempted to point to young men we know who are living their lives in much the same way as Akhom and Hassani before the attack—knowing the way of Christ but not walking in it. But let's enlarge the framework to include all ages and also look at our own walks with God. Are we willing to allow the difficulties of our lives to change us from bystanders to participants in the parade of believers around the world? Are our walks leaving footprints of faith for others to follow?

Dear Lord, our hearts are touched by the testimonies of these young men, and we thank you for them. We thank you for the healing you have brought to the bodies of Akhom and Hassani—and to their hearts. Thank you for their passion for you and how they have seen the work of your hand in the midst of painful circumstances.

Oh, God, how we need to look at the difficulties of our lives with that same lens—with the vision that only you can give and that sees with the scope of eternity. Enlarge our shortsighted vision of our lives on this earth to that higher view—your view—of an eternal perspective. Use that restored vision to revitalize our walks with you so that we will be willing to stand for kingdom purposes—no matter what the cost. Amen.

Day 33

But he knows the way that I take;
when he has tried me, I shall come out as gold.

Job 23:10

Persecution purifies the heart; like fire, it burns away dross—
anything wasteful that clings—and yields pure gold. Akhom
and Hassani are prime examples of that process when they
suffered persecution in Egypt. Their sudden decision to take
a stand resulted in the unforeseen: brutal attacks and deep-
ened walks with Christ.

While healing from their severe wounds, they reflected
on their growth in the Lord. Akhom, only twenty-one, said
the destruction of his body, which included a shattered jaw
and a now-scarred stomach, led to a renewal of his spirit.
During his time of healing, his continual prayer went

beyond the physical as he asked the Lord "to change [him], to make more perfection in [his] heart."

He is quick to point out that the pain he has suffered hasn't been without meaning. Quite the contrary, Akhom's pain has been pain with honor and follows the pattern our Lord set for us. Akhom reminds us, "He was persecuted, and he told us in this world we will suffer." And then he offers a word of hope and cheer. "But he made sure we knew he overcame the world, so we are following the same model."

Keep reminding yourself that Akhom's words are coming from a man in his early twenties: "We have to rejoice in what the Bible tells us. If persecution happens in our lives, then it is a privilege to us. It means we are going the right way."

Akhom eventually viewed the trials God had allowed for him and his cousin Hassani as a means to strengthen their faith. Hassani agrees and remains grateful for the reconstructive surgery on his face that Christians helped pay for, but he is even more grateful for God's "reconstructive surgery" on his heart.

He reflects on the miracle that he is alive because God showed him mercy. He remembers that prior to the attack, he "did not have any time to be with the Lord to pray." Now he is enjoying knowing the Lord as his "Good Shepherd" and discovering the truths of the Bible.

Two young men who had been caught up in the superficial things of the world, whose faith had been weak and untested, emerged from the fire of persecution with shining testimonies of God's grace in their lives.

Going Deeper

Where would you gauge your "fire level" for the Lord? Are you ablaze? Or is your fire of faith just barely flickering—or perhaps even a cold, gray ember? Take a thoughtful moment to sketch or write about the status of your soul flame. What would make yours burn even brighter?

Dear Lord, we are so inspired by Akhom and Hassani—by their words, their lives, their hearts for you. We marvel at the transformation that the fire of persecution produced in them. We pray for the persecuted church around the world, but today we

especially remember the young people. Thank you that you are igniting within them a passion for loving and serving you—a fire that won't be quenched. We pray for and envision a host of young people around the globe on fire for you, setting the world ablaze with your love and glory. Amen.

Day 34

For if we are beside ourselves, it is for God; if we are in our right mind, it is for you. For the love of Christ controls us, because we have concluded this: that one has died for all, therefore all have died; and he died for all, that those who live might no longer live for themselves but for him who for their sake died and was raised.

2 Corinthians 5:13–15

The scene of Sajid's torture—a man strapped to a tree and standing on a block of ice for hours while surrounded by taunting tormentors—takes us from Pakistan back to Golgotha. And both make us weep. How could they not? How could we not be moved by such great love? The incomparable love that compelled Jesus to die for us, and centuries later, the deep wellspring of love within Sajid for his Savior. A love he was willing to die for.

Sajid was a man who fearlessly followed his Lord. God had given him a dream more than a decade earlier while he was in Bible school, which directed him to Pakistan, where he led hundreds to Christ. *Hundreds!* The love and compassion of Christ had so consumed Sajid that he couldn't help but tell others about his Jesus.

What consumes you? What is so important to you that nothing—*nothing*—would deter you from that very thing? What are the things your hands may be grasping right now? Only what is worth dying for is worth living for.

Sajid knew that. He confidently told his kidnappers, "I am ready for whatever you choose to do to me. I am prepared to die for Jesus. I will not lose my passion for him no matter what you do to me."

Going Deeper

How would you answer the question "What consumes you?" Today our culture offers plenty of options for our consumption, especially with the continual advances in technology.

An indicator of what truly consumes us can often be told by the use of our time and the use of our minds. Right now think about this: What consumes us will be the wellspring we'll draw from when in dire situations. Be consumed by Jesus and his love, and you will never lack for anything.

Lord Jesus, we desire the passion that Sajid has for you. We may feel as if we fall short next to such an honorable man such as Sajid, but we know that degradation of ourselves isn't your desire for us. We also know that what you have done in Sajid you can do in us as well.

Help us to be honorable vessels for you, Lord—vessels so filled with your presence that nothing else can enter in because there simply wouldn't be any room! Those are the people we want to be, with our whole beings filled with your love and compassion. Then, no matter what presses in against us or how others pressure us, what will come out of us will be evidence of you. Amen.

Day 35

How beautiful upon the mountains
are the feet of him who brings good news,
who publishes peace, who brings good news of happiness,
who publishes salvation,
who says to Zion, "Your God reigns."

Isaiah 52:7

Think about the story of Jim and Elisabeth Elliot, missionaries to the Auca tribe in Central America. Jim and four other men lost their lives at the hands of the tribe members, but Elisabeth and her son returned there to share the gospel. Abdi of Somalia gladly joined those who place their love for Jesus and their longing for others to know him above all else.

To read Abdi's story is to read something akin to a suspense novel, and we have to remind ourselves that it is real.

His nightmare begins in his own home when four men in black awaken him with gun barrels in his face. The action moves to an underground prison cell where he is beaten. Words on a page can't convey the stench in his cell caused by the three corpses in the corner.

The bodies are replaced by two other prisoners, and the tension increases when we read of their daring escape, in which one of the men loses his life. We let out our collective breath when Abdi reunites with his family, and we rejoice when he reports that he is stronger spiritually and has led more Muslims to Christ.

We'd prefer the story to end right there. But it doesn't. Abdi, a leader in the Somali Christian community, is gunned down while driving to work. But the hail of bullets doesn't silence the heart of beauty within Abdi. It still speaks to us today.

Going Deeper

For Abdi, continuing to share the good news of Jesus was as essential as breathing. To withhold that from others was unthinkable to him. What about you? What is unthinkable to you? To play it safe with your faith or to boldly speak the truth about Jesus?

Lord Jesus, Abdi's heart for you moves us, and his love for you is beautiful. We thank you for his example of going back into the fray when it would have been easier and safer to go into hiding. Thank you that his life was not lived in vain, for many more names have been written in the Lamb's Book of Life because of his bold witness. We pray for Abdi's wife and children; comfort and strengthen them, Lord. Help them live fearlessly like Abdi, for the love and salvation of others, and we pray to join them in that pursuit. Amen.

Day 36

But he was pierced for our transgressions;
he was crushed for our iniquities;
upon him was the chastisement that brought us peace,
and with his wounds we are healed.

Isaiah 53:5

Can you think of a time in your life when something that seemed so simple and insignificant at that moment ended up becoming much more? That was the case in Algeria on a windy day in 1983—a windy day that God used to blow in the sweet breezes of Christianity in a country barren of its beauty and hope.

When some Algerian young men graciously assisted tourists in setting up their tents, they never could have dreamed the life-changing ramifications of their kind act.

The tourists responded with words of gratitude and an invitation for a congenial soccer game the next day. The group of Algerian friends decided to turn down the offer from the visitors because their best player was sick in bed with a fever.

Yet their curiosity couldn't be contained when one of the visitors asked if he and the others with him could pray for the healing of their sick friend. Nor could they squelch their astonishment when their friend was able to play soccer against the visitors the next day without a sign of his illness. Their amazement triggered questions that led to belief in Jesus.

Such simple things, for sure, when seen only on the surface: an offer of help, a response of gratitude followed by an invitation, and then an answered prayer that God used to reignite the Christian faith that had lain dormant for years in Algeria.

Going Deeper

The visitors to Algeria that memorable windy day weren't missionaries; they were ordinary folks like us enjoying a trip to another country as tourists. It is obvious that the Holy Spirit led them to engage with the young men who had helped them with their tents. Out of that initial contact, they sought friendship through a soccer game and then showed caring toward the sick friend. They met every opportunity with obedience to God's leading, never dreaming how their actions would change a country for the kingdom of God.

Today pay attention to even the seemingly small opportunities God places in your path. Respond with obedience and watch God's wonders unfold. And then do the same tomorrow, and marvel the rest of your days at how God honors a Spirit-led life.

Dear Lord, it is so easy to get caught up in our own agendas, forgetting that you may have other plans for the hours of our days. May our communion with you be so sweet and constant that we won't miss your nudges. Give us the willingness to obey even if doing so interferes with our schedules and plans.

We look forward to seeing the amazing workings of your hand as we follow your squeezes on our hearts and walk through the doors you open for us. We pray that you will strengthen our brothers and sisters in Algeria as they continue to share your love with others. Together we thank you for the joy of this adventure of following you! Amen.

Day 37

But when the chief priests and the scribes saw the wonderful
things that he did, and the children crying out in the temple,
"Hosanna to the Son of David!" they were indignant, and they
said to him, "Do you hear what these are saying?" And Jesus
said to them, "Yes; have you never read, 'Out of the mouth
of infants and nursing babies you have prepared praise'?"

Matthew 21:15–16

Do you remember being nine and in the fourth grade? See if
you can recall your teacher, your friends, your favorite activi-
ties. What are your best and worst memories of that year? The
worst thing that happened to you may seem minor in com-
parison to the turn that Hussein's life took at that age—the
day he decided to wear a cross necklace to his school in Turkey.
It wasn't a popular decision, he found out, as approximately

96 percent of the country is Muslim. His classmates spit on his necklace, swore at him, and called him an infidel.

With the unabashed enthusiasm of a child, Hussein had embraced his new faith a year earlier, following in the footsteps of his father, Hakeem, a former Islamic scholar. Then came the day Hussein decided to wear the cross as a means of telling his classmates about Jesus. The events that followed could have been a parent's worst nightmare if not for God and his purposes.

When his parents learned from his sister that Hussein had worn the cross to school, his father rebuked him, saying, "Don't *ever* tell people that you have become a Christian." He warned of the trouble that could ensue for all of them and forbade him to wear the cross again.

Fortunately, Hussein's parents soon saw the true picture: they needed to follow the example of their son and not chastise him for his boldness. From that point on, they became more open about their faith and more supportive of Hussein's outspokenness—a support much needed. The abuse at school only continued.

Although bullying has become an increasing problem in our country, it is usually one kid or a few ganging up on one student. For Hussein the whole school became his foe. From receiving threats to being shot to being jumped by a gang of boys with rocks and sticks, Hussein endured it all. Even his religious teacher beat him with a wooden rod for refusing to recite the *shahada*, the Muslim profession of faith.

Those beatings led to seizures and transfers to two different schools, where at the last school Hussein experienced fewer attacks. Yet this wise-beyond-his-years eleven-year-old is emphatic that he will never return to Islam, even if the persecutions continue. How can we argue with the truth he speaks? "Christ said we would suffer for him—we should be happy to suffer for him."

Going Deeper

Christ asks us to have the faith of a child. Hussein's story reminds us that we can have the boldness of a child too. Hussein's stand for the Lord convicted his own parents that they too needed to speak of Christ more often. Hussein is living his life in clear focus because of his faith in Jesus. Consider the role you can play for developing the faith of the children in your life. Perhaps begin by telling them the story about Hussein.

Dear God, we marvel at the wisdom and maturity of one so young who has experienced more persecution than most adult Christians in America ever have. We are reminded that you have told us that "a little child shall lead them" (Isa. 11:6). Thank you for the faith that you implant in children and how you use their precious lives of faith to embolden ours. We pray for all the Christian children in Muslim countries who have suffered so much, from the loss of their parents to the loss of their homes, leaving no food for them to eat. Help us as the worldwide church to hold them close to your heart with our prayers and to help provide for their needs. Amen.

Day 38

But recall the former days when, after you were enlightened,
you endured a hard struggle with sufferings, sometimes
being publicly exposed to reproach and affliction, and
sometimes being partners with those so treated. For you had
compassion on those in prison, and you joyfully accepted
the plundering of your property, since you knew that you
yourselves had a better possession and an abiding one.

Hebrews 10:32–34

If you have lived long enough, you have most likely had the unthinkable happen to you or to someone you love: an untimely death, disasters, divorce, chronic illness, and broken relationships rife with pain. We could fill countless volumes with sad scenarios. Our individual scripts of sorrow juxtaposed against a world steeped in horrendous events threaten to overwhelm us with all the pain—that is, if not for the difference Jesus makes.

The story of Pastor John of Maseh, Nigeria, is one that takes your breath away with its crushing sorrow. The morning of July 7, 2012, changed this minister's life forever when his church was set on fire by the mostly Muslim Fulani people. Forty-four died in that inferno, including his wife, four of his seven children, and two of his grandchildren.

How does one survive a loss so devastating? "It's painful," Pastor John said. "It was very painful. But there's nothing you can do to change the situation apart from lifting it to God."

Apart from lifting it to God. There is the secret for all of us. Pastor John did just that by going to God's Word, especially the book of Job. He gleaned sustenance from a man who had walked a similar path before him and was able to say, "In the days where there is good from the Lord, we accept it. When there is difficulty, how can we refuse to accept that?" (see Job 2:10).

Pastor John discovered that the truth of who God is doesn't disappear against the backdrop of brutal situations. Quite the contrary, against the darkness is where his light can be seen best. God and his Word don't budge an inch against any deluge of difficulties; they remain the rock-solid truth that can always be trusted.

Going Deeper

What has been the unthinkable in your life? We have seen how times of deep crisis draw people closer to God or cause them to walk away from him. There is much we don't understand in this life, but we can't let the unthinkable become the *unthankable*. As counterintuitive as it is to our human thinking, God's Word instructs us to remain thankful in everything. How is that possible? By keeping our eyes on the cross of Jesus, who did the unthinkable for us. Dwell anew on his excruciating sacrifice that ensures us eternal life—a life beyond our wildest imaginings—and offer to him your thanks in a note, poem, or song.

Lord Jesus, when we read of Pastor John's losses, we are overcome with empathy for him, our brother in Christ. Continue

to comfort his aching heart. Thank you for how that same heart has remained steadfast and sure of you in the midst of unthinkable losses. Thank you that you and your Word are ever true, ever strong, ever trustworthy. We praise you that because you are for us, nothing can come against us on this earth that we can't withstand with your strength. Praise you, dear God, for being our unmoving rock and refuge in the midst of the most unthinkable sorrows of life. Amen.

Day 39

How then will they call on him in whom they
have not believed? And how are they to believe in
him of whom they have never heard? And how
are they to hear without someone preaching?

Romans 10:14

Hussein A of Iran had decided to call it quits. Nothing in life satisfied him or made him happy. Why go on living such an insignificant life of misery? Only in his twenties, Hussein reflected on his life of using drugs and prostitutes and leading a counterfeit ring in his country. That life rang hollow with no meaning, and he was ready to make good on his decision to end it all.

Hussein had just hit the streets to buy some Ecstasy in order to have the courage to jump to his death, when an old army buddy called him. A fellow druggie, he contacted Hussein to tell him about his new discovery. Hussein anticipated hearing about a new drug that would make the jump to his demise easier. When they met for tea, never did Hussein dream that his friend was ecstatic about something totally different: Jesus.

Hours of conversation convinced Hussein to look at living life again instead of ending it. This same friend sent a Bible to him and connected him with a group of believers. When the group met in a park, where Hussein shared his story, a woman told him she too had considered suicide. And then she asked him to do what she had done herself, give all the pain to Jesus. Hussein agreed. Instead of committing suicide, he committed himself to Jesus, the one who had so radically changed his friend and given him the elusive peace he had been seeking for so long.

Hussein's army buddy didn't have to call Hussein on the day he intended to end his life. Hussein is eternally grateful his friend didn't hold back. The woman in the park didn't have to speak up either. Thank God for his intervention, and thank God for those who can't help but speak about Jesus.

Going Deeper

Write down the names of those in your circle—loved ones, neighbors, coworkers—who need to know Jesus. Pray to be used by God to make an eternal difference. Then do what he tells you. It may start with a simple phone call or a text that leads to a meaningful conversation at a coffeehouse.

Lord, we are beyond grateful for Hussein's friend and how he couldn't help but share with Hussein the best news on earth. Only eternity will tell of the ripple effect his timely phone call made, and we praise you for every person who will be in heaven because of the overflow of his joy.

Lord, we also can't help but think of all the people you have placed in our lives who still don't know you. Forgive us for caring more about what people may think of us than about where they will spend eternity. Intervene in our lives with your power and conviction so that we can intervene in the lives of others who would otherwise be headed to an eternity without you. Amen.

Day 40

I will bless the LORD at all times;
his praise shall continually be in my mouth.
My soul makes its boast in the LORD;
let the humble hear and be glad.
Oh, magnify the LORD with me,
and let us exalt his name together!

Psalm 34:1–3

Are you afraid to share your faith? Do you tend to get quiet during discussions about God? Are you prone to stick to benign topics for your Facebook posts?

We can't help but see the huge disparity, however, when we read the stories of our Muslim-turned-Christian brothers and sisters. A commitment to Christ in countries dominated by Islam can be likened to signing a death warrant, or at the least a warrant for one's arrest with subsequent beatings or other abuse. Signing a commitment card at a church service in America offers quite the contrast.

Hussein started out his faith walk in Iran quietly. He enjoyed being part of a church fellowship while continuing to enjoy the freedom of his good job and owning a home. He admits that he sensed God's call on his life for ministry but chose to decline—until the day he almost drowned. In those moments of panic in the water, Hussein asked God for one more chance and promised to minister for him.

God allowed Hussein to make good on that promise, even the one he made after his rescue: "If I have to sacrifice everything I have, I will do this." He left behind his job, got rid of his car to pay off his debts, and became an evangelist. And God honored Hussein as expressed in 1 Samuel 2:30: "For those who honor me I will honor." Hussein knew God's anointing, and many Muslims came to Christ through his compelling story. God used Hussein's near suicide to give him the courage to speak to others about the emptiness in themselves that he too had known.

Can't you just hear the conviction in Hussein's voice as he talks about having a personal relationship with God through Jesus Christ? The delight of letting others know about this God who so loves them and wants to forgive their sins? And the joy of reassuring them that this God won't withdraw his love if they make a mistake or miss a prayer?

That same delight and joy awaits you.

Going Deeper

We aren't all called to full-time ministry like Hussein, but we are called to the delight and joy of sharing Jesus with others. Where God has placed us—in neighborhoods, workplaces, and communities—is where he desires to use us in the lives of others. It might begin with a plate of cookies that could lead to the sweetness of leading another to Jesus. Is God placing someone on your heart even now? Pray for that person, and be obedient to God's leadings. You could be the one God will use to make an eternal difference.

Father, we are convicted when we think of how we are more apt to talk about everything under the sun except you, the one

who made the sun and everything else in the universe. Forgive us, dear Lord, for allowing fear to override our desire for others to know you. Help us sift the chaff from the eternal in our lives and to choose to make the changes you desire in us. We too want to honor you with our obedience. Amen.

Day 41

The apostles returned to Jesus and told him all that they had done and taught. And he said to them, "Come away by yourselves to a desolate place and rest a while."

Mark 6:30–31

We are thrilled to read how Hussein led dozens of Muslims to Christ and got involved with shipping Bibles into Iran. But surely you weren't surprised to learn how Hussein's choice to follow God's call to full-time ministry didn't come without repercussions. Shortly after a shipment of five hundred New Testaments had been delivered, eight Iranian secret police rushed in to ransack Hussein's apartment in the search for Christian literature.

Hussein and three other church leaders were taken away, and he ended up in prison after being blindfolded and shackled. We are humbled by Hussein's prayers. None was for him; his concerns were for his apartment, the Bibles there, and the welfare of the small house church.

His worries multiplied in the small, solitary confinement room with nothing but constant floodlights—no bed, no toilet, no sink. In the midst of those many worries for his coworkers and church leaders and other concerns, Hussein heard the words "Let's pray together." It was in that dark, lonely place that Jesus whispered words of comfort to Hussein and let him know there was nothing to fear.

Three days of interrogations began the next day, punctuated by kicks in the stomach for unacceptable answers. Afterward Hussein was returned to the main prison. And although God showed him amazing favor while on death row, Hussein missed being in solitary confinement. *What?* Did you wonder if you read that right? The reason Hussein gave: he preferred solitary confinement because it was easier to pray there—to commune with God—without all the distractions.

When was the last time you experienced true solitude? If you are single, that may be part of your daily existence. But when was the last time you chose solitude and silence— no music, TV, or distraction of any kind—only the pure stillness that can penetrate your soul and prepare a sacred space for listening to God?

Going Deeper

The enemy of our souls would like for us to believe his lies regarding spending time with our Lord: it is boring, unnecessary, fruitless, relatively unimportant, intimidating, and so on. Even the thought of being still in a noiseless atmosphere intimidates many. We often welcome distractions so we can ignore the deeper issues of our lives. But in silence with Jesus is where the veils can come down and intimacy with him can begin.

Dear Lord, we could easily rant about all the reasons we can't possibly take time to be alone with you. After all, you know how busy we are from morning until night with so many important things to do, right?

We confess, Lord, that we could carve out at least a few minutes a day to be with you, listen to you, hear your heart of love for us and your plan for how we can best follow you, and spend time interceding for the persecuted and for the lost. Help us, Jesus, to set apart undistracted time with you so we can learn what Hussein experienced—the beauty and joy of being in your presence. Amen.

Day 42

When Peter came to himself, he said, "Now I am sure that the Lord has sent his angel and rescued me from the hand of Herod and from all that the Jewish people were expecting."

Acts 12:11

Our Iranian brother Hussein was moved from solitary confinement to death row to join 250 other inmates. Remember, this is the same Hussein who was afraid to jump to his death, and now he was with hardened criminals who obeyed gang members over guards. Hussein's time with Jesus in solitary confinement obviously prepared him "for such a time as this" (Esther 4:14), and, like Esther, he prayed as never before.

Can you imagine his thoughts—and the contracting of his heart—when the gang members set up a midnight meeting with him in the bathroom? Don't you think he was wondering if he was going to come out of there alive? But instead of harming him, they asked for his help, convinced he had information about "his prison friends in America." Hussein was stunned and wondered if it was a case of wrong identity.

Regardless, the gang leaders were convinced and treated him like prison royalty, giving him a top bunk, a private shower, and even fresh vegetables. We can only imagine the bewilderment of the guards two days later when Hussein turned down their offer to move him to a safer part of the prison. He knew that God was showing him favor and chose to remain where God had placed him.

God's favor only continued, to the point that Hussein knew nothing to do other than shake his head in wonderment and praise God. A judge stepped in to personally oversee Hussein's case after correcting errors he found in the appeal document. And the five hundred Bibles Hussein had prayed over after his abduction were unnoticed by the police, even though they could have tripped on the boxes easily visible in the middle of Hussein's living room.

Hussein gives all praise and glory to God. He likens these events to how God opened the doors of Paul's prison cell with an earthquake. We can imagine the joy and wonder in his voice when he said, "Look how many doors God opened for me!" Yes, let us look and marvel and listen to more joyful words from Hussein: "I want to keep serving because I know God is with me."

Going Deeper

Think back to the Hussein we met at the beginning of his story—the drug addict, leader of a counterfeit ring, and frequenter of prostitutes. He was a miserable young man ready to take his own life. How can we not be transfixed by the transformation God worked in his life? Let's join together in prayer to concur with the conclusion to his story and make it our own: "They will either kill me, or there will be other miraculous events like these. Which one is bad?" Which one is bad, indeed? Are you in?

Ah, Lord, we are so inspired by Hussein's story and seeing how you intervened time and again in his difficult situation. But isn't that just like you, Lord! You respond to the heart cries of your children, just as you did for Daniel, Esther, Joseph, and many others so long ago. We praise you for being our faithful Father throughout time, the one who never changes, and the one who delights to show himself to his children. Like Hussein, we pray to know you as never before, as our Emmanuel, God with us. And we pray for hearts to gladly serve you no matter the consequences. Amen.

Day 43

Whoever finds his life will lose it, and whoever
loses his life for my sake will find it.

Matthew 10:39

Ruth and Armando's story begins with them and their three children huddled under a bridge in shallow water, which was often infested with poisonous snakes. For eight hours they waited until morning, praying not to be found by Islamic attackers.

Over the next several weeks, they and other villagers were displaced and lived in makeshift shelters to escape death. In the following five years, they would be forced to leave their homes occasionally to avoid the rebels. In two separate attacks in 2009, rebels killed four Christians and left two hundred homeless. Even today the risks are constant and real.

Yet Armando and Ruth stay because "there is a big work in this place." Where they live is "big" in its scope, both physically and spiritually. The Philippine archipelago consists of more than seven thousand islands, with about two thousand of them inhabited. The islands are divided into three large groups; Ruth and Armando live in the southernmost island group of Mindanao. It is there that the Islamic rebels wreak havoc.

One of their daughters plans to return to Mindanao to help her parents' ministry after she finishes her studies at a school of theology. Ruth is grateful to God that her daughter is willing, because Ruth wants to stay. Why? Because "God has called us here. If we die, we *die*."

Going Deeper

Are you in a hard place right now? Perhaps a relationship, a job, where you live—a host of difficult possibilities exist. Instead of asking God to remove you from that situation, ask him how he wants to use you there. He may be refining you or bringing his light to others through you—or both. He may have a "big work" for you to do right where you are.

Ruth's words echo in our minds, Lord: "If we die, we die." We don't know if we could say that with such strong resolution. Few of us are willing to put ourselves at any kind of risk of death, let alone for the sake of your kingdom. But even now you remind us how that is contrary to your Word and how it is only in the losing of our lives that we will find them—and keep them.

You are the highest example of that, dear Jesus, in how you gave up everything in order for all to be redeemed. We will never cease to praise you for such a supreme sacrifice, and we pray to exemplify you in all we do. We lift up Ruth and Armando to you. Thank you for their hearts of love for you, and we pray that you will use them and their daughter as they do a "big work" for you. Amen.

Day 44

*Not that I am speaking of being in need, for I have
learned in whatever situation I am to be content. I know
how to be brought low, and I know how to abound. In
any and every circumstance, I have learned the secret
of facing plenty and hunger, abundance and need. I
can do all things through him who strengthens me.*

Philippians 4:11–13

Walid, a young American man in his thirties, injured his ankle
and was quickly awakened to how much he took for granted.
"Even if I need to go just a few feet at work, I have to use my
crutches," he lamented. "Before, I could move and go anywhere and never thought twice about it." He was grateful that
his injury was relatively minor and temporary, and he gained a
new measure of understanding for those who can't walk freely.

Walid is one of those many people in our world today who can't move freely. Maybe you are too. Or perhaps you suffered a temporary injury in the past that gave you a renewed appreciation for your mobility. But Walid's disability wasn't caused by an accidental injury. It was the price he paid for being a Christian—a price that changed his life from then on.

Called to plant a church in Mosul, Iraq—a region embroiled in turmoil since 2003—Walid found seeking Muslims receptive to the gospel. In the face of death and destruction, they longed for peace—a longing Islam didn't satisfy. Walid continued to share the good news, and one by one, people embraced faith in Jesus. Within five months the "house church" had swelled to sixty people.

Walid's life was forever altered the day he was driving with his mother when an assailant pulled up beside them and opened fire. Three shots rang out, but a single bullet hit Walid in his spinal cord and his mother in her arm. At the hospital, Walid focused on how happy and grateful he was that his mother wasn't hurt worse and how his heart was heavy for other evangelists in Iraq working in such danger.

Today Walid continues to minister by driving a hands-only vehicle to pass out Bibles and connect with non-believers. He harbors no bitterness. His positive outlook is revealed by his words: "We all have our crosses to bear. I'm happy to bear this cross for the Lord."

Going Deeper

How would you have responded to the debilitating damage of that lone bullet if you had been the one in the driver's seat that day? Walid returned to the front line. He spoke his heart when he said, "Despite the difficult situation, the salvation of souls is taking place in big numbers in Iraq." Have you been wounded, "taken out" of ministry? Spend time with the Lord, asking him to heal your wounds and show you ways to reengage in ministry to share Christ with the lost and disciple those younger in the faith.

Thank God today for all the evangelists and house churches in Iraq, and pray that God will increase the number of believers daily.

Dear Lord, we are struck by Walid's use of the word "happy." We might be able to come to terms with bearing such a cross, but "happy" wouldn't be the word we'd use. Bearing that cross begrudgingly seems more likely. We see so much of you in Walid and his attitude, Lord, and we know that is what makes the difference. Joyful surrender to you sweetens every sacrifice. Intervene directly, Lord, to strengthen, encourage, and empower Walid and other evangelists to do your work so they can bring your truth to Iraq. Amen.

Day 45

Let me be weighed in a just balance,
and let God know my integrity!
Job 31:6

The quality of honesty is slipping in value these days. If you google the phrase "Honesty is the best policy," the first page comes up with more sites refuting the adage than concurring with it. For many, lying has become a way of life, often justified with rationale based on more lies.

In that climate of twenty-first-century thinking, we meet Hoda of Egypt. Hoda paid a price for her honesty when she was a young woman still living at home. She didn't deny to her Muslim family that she had become a Christian, so she was locked inside by her mother; her bedroom became her prison for two years. Because of her infidel status, she wasn't allowed to speak or eat with her siblings.

A few years later Hoda married Naasir, a Christian man. She and her husband continued the policy of honesty when they sought places to live in Cairo. Hoda didn't wear the traditional Muslim head covering, so they weren't hiding anything. Rather than tell a "little white lie," they always answered honestly when asked about their religious beliefs. Thirteen times they had to move because they told the truth: they were Christians.

These times of truth telling may seem small, but think about it. A life honest before God and others is honest on every level. When we choose to live in Christ, we choose to live and walk in truth. How many times have we read of our persecuted brothers and sisters refusing to renounce Christ? How many times has a truthful answer made the difference between life and death? When asked, truth is spoken: I am a Christian.

Going Deeper

Telling the truth becomes a habit. If that habit was ingrained in you during childhood, you are blessed. If you grew up in a household of lies, the lines between truth and falsity can become blurred. Yet a life of integrity, based on the teachings of the Bible, is a life that stands out, a life that stands firm. It is the life that enables you to say, "Yes, I am a Christian." Such a life points others to Jesus: the way, the truth, and the life.

Did you grow up learning to tell lies or to tell the truth? Write about that and how it has influenced your truth telling today. Then give it all to our Lord, and commit to please him by speaking truth.

Dear Lord, we confess that it is so easy these days to find ourselves on the path of the proverbial "slippery slope" of being less than honest. Often out of fear of being judged or misunderstood, we find ourselves either denying you with our silences or with outright lies. We can relate to Peter, who so regretfully denied you, and we are encouraged by how he became a rock in the faith. Thank you for the faith of Hoda and Naasir and others like them—the faith that gives them the fortitude to speak truth. We pray to emulate them, to be ever true to you, no matter what. Amen.

Day 46

For where your treasure is, there will your heart be also.

Luke 12:34

Naasir and Hoda have known the fire of persecution in Cairo, where they have been harassed and mocked for their faith, even by their families. They have known evictions, hunger, and cold—hardships that Naasir referred to as God's preparation for entrusting them with a ministry. They have also known God's provisions from when he first brought them together through Hoda's cousin. Hoda's family members were furious when they learned that she had turned her back on Islam and placed her faith in Jesus Christ. For this, they locked her in her bedroom for two years! Isolated from the rest of her family because she was an infidel, she listened to Christian radio broadcasts. When one of her cousins, a Christian, learned that Hoda was being treated like a prisoner because of her faith in Christ, he mentioned her situation to his Christian friend Naasir. Two years later, Naasir and Hoda married.

Several years and a dozen evictions later, God provided Christian workers to help them find and settle into permanent living quarters. Now an evangelist, Naasir trains others how to share God's Word. Hoda heads up a ministry dear to her heart, one that shelters women in Cairo who are forced from their homes after confessing belief in Christ.

Both are convinced they are to remain in Egypt, although they have had many opportunities to leave. Like Armando and Ruth in Mindanao, Naasir and Hoda have chosen to stay the course in Egypt for the sake of ministry, even though they are concerned about their son. His school teaches that Christians are infidels, and students are encouraged to curse Christ. Correcting these falsehoods and others is a daily task.

Despite their less-than-ideal conditions, Naasir and Hoda work out of realistic expectations framed by hope. Naasir explains, "In Egypt, our theology is the theology of pain. We don't know the theology of prosperity, but we know Jesus."

Going Deeper

If your life were stripped of everything, would your refrain echo that of our brother and sister in Egypt? *"But we know Jesus."* We came into this world with nothing, and we will leave with nothing. So even if all comes to nothing while we are still here, we can take comfort in the greatest gift of all: we know Jesus.

Do you know Jesus as well as you would like? Every close relationship requires time together. Perhaps go for a walk or find a quiet spot in your home where you can then say, "I just want to be with you, Lord." Then bask in the warmth of his loving presence, ask him for his thoughts for you, and enjoy sweet communion. It may take a while for your thoughts to quit churning, so don't leave too soon. Quiet your heart. Enjoy Jesus. *Know him.* (For best results, repeat daily.)

How can Naasir's words not grab us, Lord? We are not used to hearing about "the theology of pain," and we are not sure we want to hear about it. Once again you remind us how out of

touch we are with the rest of the world and how blessed we are to live in peace. We admire the rock-sure steadfastness of Hoda's and Naasir's faith in you, Lord. We are touched deeply by their words "But we know Jesus." In our heart of hearts, those words resonate with our desire to know you.

Help us know you better, Jesus. Deeper. More intimately. Help us know you so well that all else can fall away and it won't matter because we would still have you. Amen.

Day 47

But Jesus, knowing the reasoning of their hearts, took
a child and put him by his side and said to them,
"Whoever receives this child in my name receives me,
and whoever receives me receives him who sent me. For
he who is least among you all is the one who is great."

Luke 9:47–48

If you know someone you think is beyond the grace of God—"a hopeless case"—think again. Think of Abdulmasi, also known as "Mr. Insecticide" to his cohorts in Nigeria because of his reputation for killing "insects" or "mosquitoes," the terms he called Christians. In fact, he gloried in the killings, often returning to the scene to savor what he had done. The story of his total turnaround to follow Jesus leaves us with our mouths agape and our hearts aglow.

Forced to leave home at the age of five, Abdulmasi was sent away into the lifestyle of *almajiri*, where he, along with forty to fifty other boys, daily faced the arduous task of memorizing the Quran in Arabic. At midday the boys were sent out to beg and to bring the food first to their imam, their teacher, before eating any themselves.

Afternoons were often spent poring over the Hadith, the collection of the reports purporting to quote what the Islamic prophet Muhammad said verbatim on any matter. In those studies Abdulmasi and the other boys learned about jihad, paradise, and killing enemies of Allah. The Arabic word *jihad* is often translated as "holy war," a usage the media has popularized; but in a purely linguistic sense, it means "struggling" or "striving."

Those two words also described Abdulmasi's life: he was removed from his family to live among strangers, to study and memorize religious dogma in a language he didn't understand. All of that at the age when our children in America start kindergarten. No mother's love. No play with siblings. No guidance from a father. Just a grinding routine that Abdulmasi hated. No wonder he struck out on his own at the age of seventeen to be involved in his first jihad—to be included in taking the lives of Christians.

The little boy who missed kindergarten graduated to killing.

Going Deeper

Take a moment to look up *almajiri* on the Internet and read about how this practice is still going on today in Nigeria for *nine million boys*. While about a hundred schools have been built with better living conditions, they are in the minority. Click on the many images, look into the eyes of those young boys, and think about the difficult lives they lead, day after day. And then pray. Pray that they won't follow the path of many into terrorism, and ask what God would have you do in the life of a child. Together, one by one, we can make a difference.

Oh, dear Lord, how grateful we are that this is not the end of the story for Abdulmasi. Our hearts break when we think of

his childhood, which resembled more of a prison than a playground. And then our hearts break even more when we realize that Abdulmasi is only one of millions of little boys who are living that very life now—hurting, hungry beggars. Thank you, Father, that you see even a tiny sparrow fall and that you see these precious boys. And thank you that you don't see them as masses of millions but rather know each one by name and love them with the same amazing love that sent Jesus to the cross.

Help us, Lord, as ones who are blessed to know your love and your salvation, to seek what you would have us do to help even one needy child to know you and your love. May we, your beloved children, join together to become a mass of mercy for these broken children also beloved by you. Let it be, dear Lord. Help us make a difference for eternity in the life of a child. Amen.

Day 48

*This is my commandment, that you love
one another as I have loved you.*

John 15:12

When Abdulmasi showed up at a Christian church to become an infiltrator, he was surprised by something—the love the people showed him. The pastor and congregation welcomed him. That love never wavered, even though unbeknownst to them, Abdulmasi lived a double life for six years. One day he was a baptized Christian leading a young adult Bible study, and on another day he was a devout Muslim attending mosque to pray and fast. And on some days he would bomb yet another church across town. Six years of separate identities.

When God used a conference speaker to preach the exact words Abdulmasi needed to hear, his masks came off and all was revealed. Then he truly gave his life to Christ. Can you imagine the spectrum of emotions experienced by the fellow believers at his church? Stunned, betrayed, and understandably distrustful? Yes, they were glad that Abdulmasi had put his faith in Christ, but they thought he had done that six years earlier. What would they do with such an impostor? Would their love wane now?

What wisdom the church elders displayed in what they chose to do first. They prayed. *For three days.* God gave them their answer, and they showed their love yet again with their obedience. They chose to risk their lives for his by keeping Abdulmasi in hiding so he could live.

In Abdulmasi's words, see the difference the love of Jesus makes in his followers: "If you want to win Muslims, you have to love them, not with the human type of love but with the love you yourself have experienced through Christ."

Going Deeper

Take a few moments to reflect on the love of God. Write down words and scriptures that come to mind to describe his love and also song lyrics penned about it. How convinced are you that God's unconditional, unchanging, unlimited love is meant for you? Allow our Lord to fill every barren, hurting place within you with his healing love, and then see how he will use his love within you to touch the hearts of others.

Dear Jesus, thank you for the love you poured out on Abdulmasi, a terrorist, a killer, a sinner like all of us. Oh, how great is your love—how merciful and kind! We praise you, dear Lord, for loving us with a love so expansive and enfolding that we can barely comprehend it. Thank you that we don't have to understand your love to benefit from it.

Praise you that you have given us the privilege to be the conduits of your love to others, just like the congregation of Abdulmasi's church did for him. Help us look at every person on this planet with your eyes of love and compassion. We long to turn this hurting world upside down with your amazing love! Amen.

Day 49

*The Lord is not slow to fulfill his promise as some count
slowness, but is patient toward you, not wishing that any
should perish, but that all should reach repentance.*

2 Peter 3:9

When Abdulmasi turned fully to Christ, the pastor of his
praying, loving church told him, "My son, God is going to
use you mightily." God has fulfilled those precious words
of prophecy in Abdulmasi's life ever since. Even though
he hid in the home of another pastor, he couldn't help but
speak of his new faith to Muslims.

Not only did many Muslim men come to faith in
Christ through Abdulmasi, but he also counseled teachers
of the Quran in secret. Because of his own personal journey, his "specialty" in ministry was to reach out and help

those Muslims who were persecuting Christians. He never lost sight of how it was God's grace that had saved him and shaped him into the man he was now.

The passing of many years brought the blessings of marriage and children to Abdulmasi, yet he was never out from the shadow of the jihadists whose forces he had forsaken. In 2004 Muslims surrounded his home to kill him, but God provided a way of escape. Three years later he bore the pain of the brutal killing of his college-age son. The three Muslim men made clear their reason before they slit his son's throat: "We have come to kill you because you are your father's son."

Abdulmasi suffered deep pain because of that devastating loss, but he remained grounded in his faith, evidenced by his words: "There is no sacrifice that is too big for God." And, as God is known to do, he didn't allow death to have the last word. Abdulmasi had the opportunity to share God's love with the man who helped plan his son's death. Although he wasn't receptive, that man's son sought out Abdulmasi at his home with a seeking heart. "Please," he said, "tell me about your Christ."

Going Deeper

What loved ones do you often lift up to our Lord in prayer? How long have you been praying for them? Have you been tempted to write them off as hopeless? When you pray for them now, think of our brother in Christ, Abdulmasi, once a killer and now a giver of the good news of Jesus. How can we not pray with promise-infused hope? And when we pray for our loved ones, let's also pray for the persecuted and persecutors. Let's participate in prayer with God's mighty moving of his Spirit around the world.

Lord, how can we not marvel in awe of the orchestrations of your hand? Thank you for working wonder after wonder in Abdulmasi's life and then in turn using him in life after life. We are reminded of the apostle Paul, who also first persecuted Christians before becoming passionate about winning others to you. What a wonderful witness of your redeeming love and grace, removing any trace of doubt as far as your ability to do anything.

We think of those friends and family members who have long been on our prayer lists, some even for decades, and we pray with new faith and fervency for their salvation. Turn them to you, Lord. Soften their hardened hearts. Use whatever divinely guided means to bring them back into your loving arms. You did it for Paul and Abdulmasi, and you can do it for those we love and lift up to you now. Praise you, Jesus, for your coming answers! Amen.

Day 50

I appeal to you therefore, brothers, by the mercies of God, to present your bodies as a living sacrifice, holy and acceptable to God, which is your spiritual worship. Do not be conformed to this world, but be transformed by the renewal of your mind, that by testing you may discern what is the will of God, what is good and acceptable and perfect.

Romans 12:1–2

Didn't you love how Abdulmasi's pastor called him "my son"? Do you wonder if he had ever heard those words before? The child within us remains strong, and the boy in Abdulmasi, the little boy who grew up without a family, must have responded with gratitude and joy at the love of that father figure.

Thankfully, he also responded, with everything within him, to his heavenly Father. How else could he have endured the tragic loss of his son? When you read the words "We have come to kill you because you are your father's son," did you also catch your breath? How could we not grieve for this father? But when you now reread those words, do you see more? Do you see how they hearken back to other evil men and another Father and Son?

Jesus was killed because he claimed, rightly so, that he was God's Son. Abdulmasi's son was killed because his father spoke the truth, rightly so, about Jesus. Sacrifice upon sacrifice.

In our society the word *sacrifice* tends to carry a negative connotation—something to be avoided. You rarely hear the word in everyday conversation. But every sacrifice made for the sake of Jesus is saturated with purpose and meaning. Even the dictionary gets it right: "the surrender or destruction of something prized or desirable for the sake of something considered as having a higher or more pressing claim."* Except let's substitute "someone" for the first "something" and "Someone" for the second one. Jesus, indeed, has a higher—*the highest*—claim on our lives. He is the one worth every sacrifice on this earth.

Going Deeper

The Christians being persecuted for their faith in Muslim countries aren't surprised by the reality of sacrifice in their lives. "After all," they would have every right to say to us, "the Bible has told us we would be persecuted. It is an honor to suffer for Christ."

Have you noticed how easy it is to rush through those particular Bible passages or skip over them altogether?

Our brothers and sisters have counted the cost, and they willingly offer themselves to Jesus every day, always living with the knowledge that they may pay the ultimate sacrifice with their lives. What about you? Have you counted the cost? Are you willing to sacrifice everything, if need be, for the cause of Christ? Gather your family in this decision, and

---

*   Dictionary.com, s.v. "sacrifice," http://dictionary.reference.com /browse/sacrifice?s=t.

together determine to follow Jesus, only and always, no matter what doing so may demand.

Lord, we stumble in our feeble understanding of sacrifice. We often look upon it as some material thing we have to give up, even for a short time. Yet when we raise our eyes to you, Jesus, and see you on the cross, the word "sacrifice" crystallizes. It is you, Lord. You are the supreme sacrifice, the final sacrifice, the for-all-time sacrifice that brings never-ending praise to our hearts and lips. Thank you, our Savior! Thank you for enduring the cross so that we can live eternally with you.

Help us see daily that any sacrifice required by us is simply a love offering to you. Enable us to encase every sacrifice with joy and to lift each one up to you with hearts of praise. May the extraordinary sacrifices of our brothers and sisters worldwide inspire us and ignite us to follow their examples of unflinching devotion to you. Amen.

Day 51

And these words that I command you today shall be on your heart. You shall teach them diligently to your children, and shall talk of them when you sit in your house, and when you walk by the way, and when you lie down, and when you rise. You shall bind them as a sign on your hand, and they shall be as frontlets between your eyes. You shall write them on the doorposts of your house and on your gates.

Deuteronomy 6:6–9

Sometimes older people don't feel significant as they age, especially in our youth-obsessed culture in America. Yet the impact and influence of a loving and godly older adult should not be diminished. In the case of Yousef, a young Muslim man in the Middle East, God used a story his grandfather had told him years earlier to save his life.

The storytelling came about in a casual way while Yousef was sitting on his grandfather's lap during a television program. The documentary demonstrated how salmon swim upstream against the flow, and his grandfather turned that fact into a teachable moment for his young grandson. He likened Christians to the salmon, letting Yousef know that they always had to swim against the current. But, he emphasized, it was that effort, all that energy, that kept them full of life, unlike the "fish" that take the easy route downstream—those of the world—and die.

The memory of that story touched Yousef deeply on a night he desperately needed a touch from God—so deeply that he decided to temporarily set aside the bottle of pills that he had planned to take to end his life. He pleaded with God—his grandfather's God—for Jesus to reveal himself by the end of the next day, and then he wouldn't take his life.

Yousef awoke the next morning to find his uncle sitting on the end of his bed, a direct answer to his prayers, he realized later. His uncle wanted to talk to Yousef about Jesus, the one his father (Yousef's grandfather) had led him to after his own wanderings. His uncle explained how in his youth he dismissed his dad and his talk about Jesus and became a drug smuggler. But when his world crumbled, he remembered the contentment in the life of his father, who eventually led him to Jesus.

Yousef was drawn to his uncle's story and talked to him regularly about Jesus. His uncle eventually gave him a Bible. Yousef's Muslim mother, a female leader in the local mosque, became his most formidable foe in his quest for faith, but he still resolved to give his life to Jesus.

God used a story told to a little boy on his grandfather's lap to save that boy's life now and for all eternity. Yousef's grandfather had moved to America years earlier, but he left behind in the Middle East his legacy of faith—a legacy that still lives on even though the grandfather is now with his Lord.

Going Deeper

Jesus often told stories to illumine deeper truths. Prayerfully seek to be attuned to God-given moments of opportunity for telling stories of faith and hope to future generations. Look for even ordinary moments to convey truth and leave a legacy of love where God has placed you.

Around the world, Lord, in the lives of your children, you often use the simplest of things to proclaim your love. Thank you for making your way of truth so simple that even children can easily grasp your love for them. Thank you for the obedience of Yousef's grandfather, who gives us a worthy example of how a righteous man's steps are ordered by you. Thank you for using his influence in the lives of both his son and his grandson and for generations to come to show forth your truth to Muslims in the Middle East. Help us emulate his example and, with your help, Lord, point others to you. Amen.

Day 52

*Count it all joy, my brothers, when you
meet trials of various kinds.*

James 1:2

How do you enjoy spending your Sundays, the day God set aside for worship and rest? Parveen, a young woman in Pakistan, especially looked forward to Sunday; it was her only day off from work. But even better than that, Sunday was when she could attend church and then be with her family at home, where they often enjoyed reading the Bible together.

The other six days of Parveen's week were spent working as a maid while living in a Muslim home. Her wages? Seventeen dollars a month in US dollars, and some of that helped support her family.

Then came the Saturday when her boss insisted she work on a Sunday to help with guests. When Parveen refused to give up her one day off, citing that it was her day to go to church and "her family's special day," the persecution behind closed doors began. Slaps, punches, and kicks. Mocking her faith. Trying to bribe her. Torturing her for hours, including burning her wrists with cigarettes. Locking her in a room for two days with little food and no water. Even in the midst of that abusive situation, Parveen spoke words of faith about her Jesus.

This isn't the image of a line of men in orange on a lone beach about to be publicly beheaded for their faith, but Parveen's situation is indicative of what goes on for many Christians in Muslim countries. Even when Parveen's parents tried to check on her, they were turned away with excuses until they eventually were able to bring their twenty-three-year-old daughter back home.

And just as he did with Joseph of Bible times, God fulfilled a dream he gave Parveen and brought good out of her prison-like existence. Her dream? To offer new opportunities to young Christian women stuck in similar conditions. God opened that door when other Christians provided her with a sewing machine; now Parveen teaches women to sew so they can support themselves from home. Free from fear of torture and abuse in a Muslim home, Parveen views her home workplace as much more than her workplace; it is also her place of worship and prayer.

Going Deeper

When Parveen was offered one hundred thousand rupees from her Muslim employer to "satisfy [her] family's needs," if only she would accept Islam, she didn't hesitate to respond. "If you offer me ten billion rupees," she said, "I will not accept Islam." From what reservoir did Parveen draw that kind of courage and confidence? Perhaps the one filled by years of Sundays spent reading the Word with her family? Perhaps hours spent memorizing Scripture? If you don't already have a daily routine, commit now to spending time in God's Word consistently and walking with his truth.

Lord, we take so much for granted, easily forgetting how different things are around the world. Thank you for using Parveen's story to remind us to pray for those many Christians suffering in silent persecution. The stories of their persecuted existence may not make the headlines, but many are living in miserable situations and are sustained only by your grace. We pray for them right now, Jesus. Give them every needed gift of mercy from your hand. Give them courage and perseverance and an ever-growing faith in you, grounded in your Word. Give them your measureless peace. Amen.

Day 53

You make known to me the path of life;
in your presence there is fullness of joy;
at your right hand are pleasures forevermore.

Psalm 16:11

Over and over we hear a recurring word used by Muslims—even very devout Muslims—when they tell of their lives before coming to Christ: *empty. Empty*—desolate, unfilled, wanting. That was Sara as a young woman in Iran who could have been the poster child for a devout young Muslim.

A member of an elite Islamic group and a known prayer warrior, Sara was esteemed by other girls. From extreme fasting to self-flagellation, Sara did all she knew to do to fill the void within her, but nothing replaced the aching vacancy in her heart. Although religious, she lacked a relationship with the true God. She longed for that connection, and her life felt devoid of purpose and meaning.

That condition continued until her sister came home from college with a movie about the life of Jesus, the tool God used to show Sara what—or who—was missing from her life: Jesus. Through that video she came to Christ. When she prayed, God let her know that he was the truth and the one and only true God. Her conversion led to meeting secretly with a house church. The highlight was receiving a New Testament, a treasure in a country that has few Bibles.

Sara wasn't content to keep her now inhabited and satisfied heart to herself. The bus to and from work became her vehicle—literally!—for sharing the good news of Jesus. While she knows it is risky, she delights in witnessing to women, knowing that the men on the other side of the dividing rail are also listening. Her daily commute is when she communicates the love of Jesus and tells how he filled her empty heart to overflowing.

Going Deeper

Do you know what it is like to feel empty, as Sara and others have described? Have you opened your heart wide to Christ so he can fill you with all the fullness of himself? It is interesting to note the hope-filled antonyms for the word *empty*: *Sufficient, abundant,* and *replete. Cherished* and *animated. Fruitful, complete,* and *effective.* What words describe the status of your heart today?

Jesus, how our hearts rejoice that Sara now knows you! Thank you for filling her with yourself and releasing her from a life of meaningless religiosity. You have made our hearts to yearn for connection with you, and you are faithful to draw near to those who draw near to you. Thank you for being the one and only true and faithful God, who loves us deeply and yearns for a relationship with us. There is nothing sweeter than that constant heart-to-heart communion with you, Jesus, that adds richness and depth to our days like nothing else.

Be with Sara on her daily commute and protect her. Use her in the lives of Muslims so that they too can know the joy and fulfillment of a true relationship with you. Thank you that Sara loves you so much she can't help but speak of you. May our love for you abound in the same way, Lord, so that we will take joy in sharing you at every opportunity. Amen.

Day 54

Jesus looked at them and said, "With man it is impossible,
but not with God. For all things are possible with God."
Mark 10:27

Hopeless is not found in God's vocabulary. We, however, are too familiar with it, succumbing to our tendency to look at circumstances instead of keeping our eyes fixed on Jesus. With God nothing is hopeless, nothing is impossible. Samrita would heartily agree, as she has seen verifiable proof that still amazes her.

Growing up in Malaysia, Samrita had twelve siblings and a father who was owned by alcohol. He told them all how worthless they were and hit them. The physical abuse hurt and bloodied Samrita, but it was the unkind words that shredded her soul during her childhood and teen years.

Like many young women in similar situations, Samrita escaped by means of a marriage, even though she had to convert to Islam to do so. And then she found herself in the same nightmare, with a man who went down the path of drugs and beat Samrita, his wife. At a friend's suggestion, she upped her religious practices in Islam, hoping to find the peace that eluded her. But nothing helped.

And then her help came from the very one who had been her childhood nemesis, the enemy to her happiness: her father. When he came back into her life one day, she hardly knew whether to believe his words of becoming a Christian—and thus a changed man. But it didn't really matter if she believed his words, because his actions in the coming months proved them to be true.

She could no longer recognize the angry bully who had once been her father, because he now emanated gentleness and kindness. He was the personification of the "new creation" in Christ, with the old truly gone and the brand new in its place. As he did with all his children, he asked Samrita to forgive him. The gift he gave her, a necklace of a small wooden cross, represented the gift God gave to her—a redeemed father.

Going Deeper

Ponder these words by Samrita's father when he told her he had become a Christian: "I have left my anger, my ego, and my stupidity at the foot of the cross." And he obviously gained humility when he left all that was caused by pride. Take some time to think and pray about whether there is anything you need to leave at the foot of the cross today. What "newness" will you welcome in exchange for what you leave? Express your praise to God for his precious gifts of redemption.

Lord, we know the truth of your Word and how you make all things new, but now and then we need to hear it again. Thank you for this poignant reminder you have given us through Samrita's story. We praise you that no one is hopeless—no one is beyond the reach of your redeeming power. Thank you for restoring and healing this family once so wounded. We pray for the same healing of hurts in families we know, perhaps even our own. Help us never to put limits

on you, Lord. Help us not to give up on praying for your breakthroughs. Help us keep our eyes fixed on you alone, the giver of hope and the one who makes all things possible. Amen.

Day 55

For I consider that the sufferings of this present time are not worth comparing with the glory that is to be revealed to us.

Romans 8:18

The transformation of Samrita's father was unlike anything she had ever seen, and it triggered many questions for her about Jesus and Christianity. She couldn't ignore the miracle of her father's countenance and behavior changing from anger to peace, and she wanted to know the source. So she asked questions, and God worked in her life with his answers. Samrita found the peace her father exuded when she too accepted Christ as her Savior at a Christian seminar she attended in 2008.

Not wanting anything to negate her newfound peace, Samrita chose not to tell her Muslim husband, Uda. But the day he found her Bible is the day he kicked her out of the house; she left with their two children, ages ten and five. Uda divorced her, and her future ended up in the hands of the Shariah police, the administrators of Islamic law.

She now faced being sentenced to three years at a detention center if it was reported that she had left Islam. If she refused to enter the rehabilitation center, she could face prison. But God's people fasted and prayed, and he mercifully intervened. The judge granted the divorce and gave the children to Uda, with no visitation rights for Samrita. But she was left in freedom, and as time passed, Uda allowed her to visit their children. She has been warned by Uda and the court not to share her faith with the children, but how can she not give them words of truth and life when she has those windows of opportunity? And so she does.

Samrita longs for her children and prays that God will open the door for her to have her children live with her once again. In the meantime, she is involved in a church of sixty other believers in Malaysia and enjoys a close relationship with her father. Saying she is "willing to suffer for Christ," Samrita lives each day serving him in appreciation of the truth she has witnessed: "All things have become new" (see Rom. 5:17).

Going Deeper

Rare is the Christian in a Muslim country who doesn't pay a daily price—up to the ultimate price of life itself—for being a follower of Christ. Fairness doesn't fit into the equation of faith. The cost of Samrita's faith is the forfeiture of the joy and privilege of raising her children and teaching them about Jesus. What is your faith costing you? Consider listing all the ways you are free to live out your faith, and then thank God for each aspect.

Lord Jesus, our hearts go out to Samrita in her daily suffering of separation from her beloved children. We can't imagine children being yanked away from a parent because of profession of faith in you. Thank you that your divine love and care for Samrita's children far surpasses even her deep motherly love. Keep them close to your heart, Lord, and protect their minds and hearts in every way. Use them in the life of their father, Uda, to bring him to know you. What you did in the life of Samrita's father you can do in the life of Uda. Comfort Samrita and keep her

strong in you, full of faith and anticipation of the day when all things will become new on the new earth. We praise you, Lord, that every promise you give proves true. Help us live in that wonderful reality today. Amen.

Day 56

For my thoughts are not your thoughts,
neither are your ways my ways, declares the Lord.

Isaiah 55:8

Every realm of life reveals God's creative perfection and attention to detail. Study the seas, the human eye, or the starry skies, and each one will lead you to greater awe of God, the original designer. Observe hummingbirds and ladybugs and butterflies against the backdrop of a garden with flowers of every hue and scent, and you can't help but see how God infuses beauty with his creativity.

God's creativity certainly spills over into the lives of those of us made in his image. His use of a talking donkey with Balaam and a huge fish with Jonah display his willingness to employ unusual ways to get our attention. Afrooz, a frazzled college student in Iran, learned that truth in the midst of trying to balance school and work while battling doubts about her Islamic faith. One night at a point of desperation, she called out to Allah, "If you are going to help me, tonight you should show yourself to me. If you don't show me a sign tonight, I will turn to this material life and be a sinner."

Later, when her room flooded with light at midnight, she saw the true God's answer: his Son. When she saw the Man in white, she immediately knew he was Jesus the Messiah. The student in her grabbed some paper and a pen to write down what he might say. Yet the words he spoke only angered her, as she had no context to give them meaning.

The next night, Jesus met with her again in a vision, but it only added to her confusion. Why was she seeing Jesus instead of Allah or Muhammad? God didn't leave her mystified for long. When a coworker encouraged her about another concern with the biblical counsel "God is love" and "God is always with you," he let her know he was a Christian.

Stunned, Afrooz told him the events of the past two nights, including the words Jesus spoke. He pulled out his

Bible and showed her the very same words in Matthew 11:28: "Come to me, all who labor and are heavy laden, and I will give you rest." God's creative orchestrations and words of truth led Afrooz straight into the welcoming arms of Jesus.

Going Deeper

Every sunrise and sunset is God's call to see him. Carve out some time today under the sky's canopy and meditate on Psalm 8. Praise God for his marvelous and creative workings in this world and in the lives of his children, including Afrooz and you.

Lord, what a wonderful story of your grace! We are without words grand enough to express our wonder and praise to you. The most ardent adjectives in every language combined still fail and fall short in giving adequate praise to you. Your thoughts and ways are so high and lofty; we love you and your creative ways! Thank you for hearing Afrooz when she called

out to a false god and for pursuing her until she responded to your loving overtures.

O Lord, our Lord, how excellent, how majestic are your ways in all of the earth! Praise you! Help us lift you up so that all will be drawn to you, the one who is worthy of all praise and honor. Amen.

Day 57

Then he said to them, "But who do you say that I am?" And Peter answered, "The Christ of God."

Luke 9:20

When Afrooz saw her second vision of Jesus, Jesus did the same thing he was known for when he walked this earth—he asked a question: "Didn't I tell you to come under my shadow and come with me and be safe?"

When Afrooz believed God to be her safe place, she was freed to live out her faith even under much opposition. It began when she sought a different job and learned of the hostility toward Christians that showed up in lower pay and no insurance or benefits.

When she married the Christian man she met at church, their wedding night was marred by the questioning of the Iranian secret police when they arrived at their hotel. The police pelted them with questions about their church and pastor, and wanted to see proof of their marriage. That troubling incident became the impetus for their move to northern Iran, where they both got involved in fulfilling ministries. After they named their baby daughter the Christian name of Emmanuel—*God with us*—the harassment resurfaced, forcing them to move on yet again.

It hasn't been easy for their family to be uprooted due to the terrible things that could happen because of their faith. But Afrooz had accepted Jesus's invitation years earlier to come under his shadow, to come with him. She accepted his promise that *he* would be her safe place.

Going Deeper

A woman seeking God's guidance tossed and turned in bed as thoughts whirled in her mind, robbing her of sleep. God had given her many indicators to believe a certain way for a major need in her life, but it would take a miracle to bring it about—a miracle she couldn't even imagine. She wanted to believe him, but it seemed too impossible, and that is when she felt his reassuring presence in the darkness, accompanied by a question: "Why should you doubt?" Suddenly a wave of memories washed over her of God's many provisions over the years as she heard some gentler words: "Do not doubt." A restful sleep soon followed.

What question is Jesus asking you lately? Or maybe it is a question he asked you long ago. The more important question is, what is your response? When you respond in faith or obedience to whatever Jesus asks of you, that is *always* the right answer.

Lord, we praise you again for how you so amazingly brought Afrooz out of her distress and into your salvation in such a dramatic and convincing way. Yet living for you and serving you hasn't come without its hardships. We pray for Afrooz, her husband, and their daughter, wherever they are in Iran right now. We ask that you will give that precious family a refreshing sense of your presence that will strengthen their spirits. Keep them looking up to you, and keep us praying

for them and others like them. And help us remember that your every question to us is asked in love and accompanied by your reassurances. May we glorify you with a response of obedience. Amen.

Day 58

But the fruit of the Spirit is love, joy, peace, patience, kindness, goodness, faithfulness, gentleness, self-control; against such things there is no law.

Galatians 5:22–23

Do you wake up every morning excited to jump into your day? Not so much? Boutros of Syria does, and his enthusiastic joy in Jesus is contagious even via the printed page. Duty isn't demanding him to share Jesus with everyone he meets; delight is. Legalism isn't his motivation; love is.

Living in a village outside of one of Syria's major cities, Boutros ventures out into the streets to persuade others to trust in Jesus. We can't help but surmise that his heart for Christ lights up his countenance as he gives out Bibles and shares his faith.

That is what he was doing when he didn't come home one day, even though a 4:00 p.m. curfew had been imposed. A church leader had spoken to him just days earlier about his boldness, warning him about the kidnapping and torture—to the point of Christians being cut into pieces. "We cannot afford to lose you," he pleaded.

But Boutros could hear only God's summon. "But this is what I'm called to do—to spread the good news of Christ to thirsty Syrians."

As the absence of Boutros moved into a full day and then another, his church friends, gathered as a congregation, continued to cry out to God for his safety while they battled mental images of his possible demise.

When Boutros finally walked through the church doors, his friends learned that nothing could stifle him, not even being picked up by the secret police. Instead of going away after they released him, he went one block over to a shop-lined street to share the life-giving news of Jesus. That landed him in jail, where he conversed with Muslim extremists who wanted to know why he was there. What a perfect opener for Boutros to share the passion of his heart—the love of Jesus.

Later he looked the head officer of the secret police in the eye and told him the best news on earth, the news that compels Boutros to continue to follow God's call on his life: "God is love. And he loves you."

Going Deeper

Joy stems from knowing Jesus as our dearest friend and is God's magnet to draw others to him and his love. The words we speak resonate more deeply when they are punctuated with joy. Want more joy in your life? Spend time with Jesus and his Word, enjoy his endearing presence, and joy will naturally result. Don't be surprised when friends, neighbors, and coworkers ask, "Why are you always so joyful?" Then be ready to respond, "It's because of Jesus in my life!"

Lord, Boutros's joy and love for you are so infectious! Oh, how we long to love you like that—with a love so unfettered, so free, so irrepressible! No wonder he can't help but talk about you and your love when he himself is so consumed by that very love.

That is the key, isn't it, Lord? To really know you and your love. What becomes our personal story of being so loved, so forgiven, so free then becomes the best news on earth that we simply have to share with everyone. Help us, our Lord, to so embrace your life-changing love that our hearts for you won't be held hostage in any way as we share you with unhampered joy. Amen.

Day 59

Have I not commanded you? Be strong and courageous.
Do not be frightened, and do not be dismayed, for
the Lord your God is with you wherever you go.

Joshua 1:9

The teen years are often filled with turmoil and angst, no matter the culture or the country of residence. Although the faces may be diverse, the hearts of teens mirror each other in their musings and questions: *Why am I here? Do I matter? Does anyone truly love me for who I am? What am I to believe? What is truth?*

Amal's questioning journey began when she was a thirteen-year-old Muslim girl in Israel struggling with where she fit in the world around her. In her quest for answers, she came to a crossroads. She didn't know which direction led to the truth she was seeking. Can you relate? Perhaps you did what Amal did at that point: she prayed.

Reminiscent of the showdown between the prophets of Baal and the true God of Elijah in 1 Kings 18, Amal needed to know the impostor from the real. She called on God, beseeching him to reveal himself to her either as the god of Islam or as the God of Christianity. She vowed to wear the head covering and say the prayers if he were the god of Islam. But her next sentence demonstrated the depth of her searching and her desire for solid answers: "But if you are the God of Christians, even if this will lead me to be killed, I will still believe in you."

In the same way as God has often answered other sincere seekers in Islamic countries, he answered Amal in a dream. The light of Jesus was so bright she couldn't look at it. Jesus walked with her in the dream, pulling her up every time she fell, until they came to an oasis. He told her the answer she was looking for was in the book he had her retrieve out of the water, and in it she read, "I am the way, and the truth, and the life."

Then she awoke, wondering where those words came from—the Quran, the Bible, where? In her diligent searching, she learned the answer: John 14:6 in the Bible. That night she upheld her promise and believed fully in Jesus.

Going Deeper

Amal's young heart for God is remarkable, especially in a world where teenagers often rank fame as their number one goal. Amal chose the significant and substantive over the shallow and superficial. What can we learn today from this young woman's life, no matter our age?

Lord, Amal's words echo in our ears: "Even if this will lead me to be killed, I will still believe in you." What resolve she had to follow you, even if it meant her death at the age of thirteen. We love you, Lord, and we too want to commit to following you even to the point of death, but we admit we are not sure if we could do it. Not sure if we are strong enough. Not sure if our lives were threatened that we could be fearless in our faith.

Thank you for reminding us that we don't need to know that now. All we need to know is that we are willing to follow you on whatever path you have for us this moment, this day. Thank you for your assurance that whatever lies ahead, you will precede us and give us the necessary faith to follow you, one step at a time. Amen.

Day 60

Then the righteous will shine like the sun in the kingdom
of their Father. He who has ears, let him hear.

Matthew 13:43

Amal's decision to follow Jesus was not met with fanfare and rejoicing in her family, as one might see in America. The opposite is always true in Muslim families when someone converts to Christianity, with the spectrum of disapproval ranging from being ignored to being murdered. Amal suffered abuse not only from her parents but also from her older brother.

Her mother made a habit of finding and burning Amal's Bibles, nine in all. Her father joined her brother in beating her, causing her to faint and the father to have a stroke. Because Amal was deemed the cause of her father's stroke, she was confined to her room and given little food to eat. Difficulties continued, but she honored God in them all.

What came out of her unwavering stand for Christ? God enabled her to move out and go to a Bible school. When her father learned of her graduation from there, he shunned her for two months. But God is always at work, even when his workings are invisible to us. Amal moved back home, and God moved on the hearts of her family. Three sisters and a younger brother came to Jesus. Her parents have even accepted Amal's faith, although they have yet to embrace it for themselves.

And what about the older brother who beat her? He is now married, but he still wields his threats: "I am just waiting to do something to hurt you."

As for Amal, she continues to serve the God who answered the plea of her thirteen-year-old heart. She leads a group of people in their twenties who also have chosen the living God of the Bible over the deadening claims of Islam. They too are following Jesus, the way, the truth, and the life.

Going Deeper

How easy and natural it is for us to pray only for the concerns contained within our circle of family and friends. Today let's enlarge that circle to include the entire world and focus on the fact that our family in Christ lives everywhere. Place sticky notes or pushpins on a globe or map as your prayer reminders, and be faithful to praying for our persecuted brothers and sisters and for those coming to their aid.

Lord, when we think of our sister Amal in Israel and her faith journey, you remind us of when we were that tender age of thirteen. Amal had so many questions, so many uncertainties, so many challenges, and so many different directions she could have gone. But she chose to seek you, and true to who you are, our faithful Lord, you chose to answer her. Thank you for undeniably proving to Amal that you alone are the only God, the only one worthy of our worship and praise.

We praise you for Amal's siblings who have also professed faith in you. Oh, the ripple effect of your grace! We thrill to think of how so many others will come to know you because of Amal's firm faith in you. We pray that you will continue to use Amal in the lives of many as she shines for you. We especially pray for her dear parents and older brother, who desperately need you, Jesus. Remove the blinders from their eyes so that they may clearly see you and join their family in joyous confession of you as their Savior. We look forward to seeing Amal and her entire family in heaven one day. Praise you, Lord! Amen.

Day 61

*And Jesus said, "Father, forgive them, for
they know not what they do."*
Luke 23:34

Danjuma was only thirteen when nearly a thousand
Islamic insurgents invaded his village in Nigeria early one
Wednesday morning. The horrendous attack left in its wake
the death toll of twenty-three Christians, with thirty-eight
more injured. Everyone still marvels that Danjuma's name
didn't land on the list of the dead, based on the atrocities
done to his body that day. A machete slashed the left side of
his head and arm, while a knife gouged out his right eye and
cut off his testicles.

How can we not recoil in horror when we hear of such
heinous deeds inflicted on innocent people, including

children? A "righteous anger" rises up within us, which is often challenging for us to keep "righteous." In truth, many of us would cheer with joy—whether secretly or openly—to see retribution against the butchers who committed such barbaric acts.

But wait. What is the stance of Danjuma? What does he say about the murderers who tried to massacre him? The words of this now one-eyed boy give us incredible insight into his heart: "I forgive them because they don't know what they are doing." His compassion for these killers confounds us when he adds, "If they had love, they wouldn't behave that way."

Today Danjuma's smile radiates so brilliantly that it outshines the scars on his mutilated face. Only Jesus could bring such a glow in the aftermath of such a grisly event.

Going Deeper

Are you tempted to respond with revenge rather than offering forgiveness toward the brutal killers who terrorized Danjuma's village? Think about Danjuma's words, "If they had love, they wouldn't behave that way."

As difficult as it may be, try to picture those men as babies, toddlers, and young boys, and imagine their childhoods. Did they ever know love? Or were they given up by their families at a young age to be indoctrinated with hateful dogma and desensitized to violence and killing? Have they ever been told of the love of Jesus? We can't know any of that for sure. But we do know that they are part of "the world" that Jesus talked about God loving in John 3:16. Our impartial God loves them as much as he loves anyone. That truth alone compels us to pray for them with loving compassion.

Our Lord, we fall on our faces before you in humility and repentance. The words of Danjuma pierce us to the core, in the best of ways. We see in him you, dear Jesus—your love, your compassion, your forgiveness. And we know that all those gifts from your hand come together to create his amazing countenance of joy.

Thank you for Danjuma. Thank you for saving his life so he can speak into the hearts of many—hearts like ours, Lord.

Use Danjuma to remind us what forgiveness looks like, to see the difference you make, to make us want to imitate him as he imitates you. Continue to heal Danjuma in every way, and give us hearts of forgiveness to look like his. Amen.

Day 62

But I trust in you, O LORD;
I say, "You are my God."

Psalm 31:14

Trials and hairbreadth escapes only strengthened my
faith and nerved me for more to follow; and they trod
swiftly enough upon each other's heels. Without that
abiding consciousness of the presence and power of my
Lord and Saviour, nothing in the world could have
preserved me from losing my reason and perishing
miserably. His words "Lo, I am with you alway, even
unto the end" became to me so real that it would
not have startled me to behold Him, as Stephen did,
gazing down upon the scene. It is the sober truth that
I had my nearest and most intimate glimpses of the

presence of my Lord in those dread moments when
musket, club or spear was being leveled at my life.
John G. Paton (1824–1907), missionary from Scotland
to the New Hebrides Islands of the South Pacific

Godly traits are most often gained in the trenches of trials. Read books such as *Foxe's Book of Martyrs* and biographies of strong believers and you won't find the stuff of fairy tales or comedy sitcoms. But you will read amazing responses to their trials—responses that honor and glorify God. You may know someone personally who has responded to severe trials with grace and joy.

Danjuma, the thirteen-year-old from Nigeria, would easily fit into that category. Here was a boy left for dead—a boy who, in light of his dire situation, should have died. Add to the severity of his machete and knife wounds the fact that the hospital was fifteen miles away from his village. He should have bled to death. But God had a different plan.

God's intervention in Danjuma's life birthed a nickname for him: Miracle. But that name extends beyond Danjuma's amazing survival and physical recovery. We see in Danjuma's heart the miracle God can work in any heart—the miracle of a heart like his. Despite all the trauma he suffered, when Danjuma looks back on what happened to him, he simply says, "There is no problem. I have allowed God to handle everything."

Going Deeper

Were you astounded to read Danjuma's words about there being "no problem"? And were you inspired by his words "I have allowed God to handle everything"? This teen's "everything" included forgiving the men who tried to kill him and dealing with challenging physical problems for the rest of his life.

Think about your "everything"—every concern troubling you. With words or sketches, "list" each one, and then lift them up to God with a prayer of relinquishment so that you can say with Danjuma, "I have allowed God to handle everything."

Oh, Lord, when we give in to our tendency to gripe and complain about our problems, please remind us of dear Danjuma.

Thank you for his tender heart toward you and for what he can teach us. The attitude and heart-set of this, your child, both inspire and convict us. And that is a good thing, Lord, because our hearts long to be what we see in your servants such as Danjuma: to be more like you. More loving. More compassionate. More forgiving.

Help us to renounce self-reliance and instead fully depend on you, trusting that you will handle everything in our lives too. Keep Danjuma and his shining testimony alive in our hearts, and allow his triumphant voice to be heard around the world in victory and praise. Amen.

Day 63

Jesus said to her, "Everyone who drinks of this water
will be thirsty again, but whoever drinks of the water
that I will give him will never be thirsty again.
The water that I will give him will become in him
a spring of water welling up to eternal life."

John 4:13–14

Do you remember a time when you were parched with thirst to the extreme, with no water available to you? All you could think about was relieving your thirst, right? And then do you recall the exquisite joy of that first gulp of water that you had been longing for?

An unrelenting thirst led Jamil to embark on a search for spiritual truth. Raised in a moderate Muslim home in a country south of Russia and north of Iran and Afghanistan,

Jamil began his search after his brother's more radical beliefs landed him in prison. Jamil's studies and soul-searching intersected with meeting some Christians who shared the good news of Jesus with him.

With the exposure to the gospel, Jamil drank in truth after truth. Jesus was the one true God—everything that Allah wasn't. Jesus was the Messiah, the Promised One, the Savior. Jamil's thirst was finally satisfied!

What else could he do then but bring everyone he loved to the streams of living water found only in the Lord? That brother who had become an extremist? Jamil led him to Christ—and three other siblings as well. The thirst-quenching truth he had discovered continued to flow out of Jamil, and he planted four house churches.

Just as the woman at the well couldn't wait to share with her village about Jesus, Jamil knew that same eagerness to tell everyone about the "spring of water welling up to eternal life." His thirst had been satisfied, and so great were his appreciation and gratitude that they overflowed into the lives of others.

Going Deeper

Do you know anyone "thirsting" for truth and meaning in life—thirsting for Jesus? That thirst and desire for the Lord is often disguised by people's ability to wear masks and appear satisfied. Most would be surprised to discover that Jesus is at the heart of their longing. Ask the Lord to reveal the parched souls around you, and be blessed to offer the living water of Jesus with joy.

Jesus, thank you for Jamil and how he reminds us that a life without you is truly a desert for the soul. We are ever so grateful for the life we enjoy that is found in you alone. Thank you for leading Jamil to your truth and for the many he has led to you, the Living Water. Help us look around us—beyond us—and clearly see the parched souls of others. Use us to be free-flowing channels of your living water so that others can know the truth of life everlasting in you. Amen.

Day 64

You have heard that it was said, "You shall love your neighbor and hate your enemy." But I say to you, Love your enemies and pray for those who persecute you, so that you may be sons of your Father who is in heaven. For he makes his sun rise on the evil and on the good, and sends rain on the just and on the unjust.

Matthew 5:43–45

The will to endure beatings almost every night for three years requires a supernatural grace. But that is what Jamil did after he married, had a son, and accepted an offer to minister to a Central Asian village filled only with Muslims. When the word got around about this newcomer and infidel, they showed up at Jamil's door and the beatings began.

Jamil would quote Scripture to his attackers but refused to fight back. After they would leave, he would wash his bloodied face, willing to pay the price for being hated because of his faith in the Lord he loved. But the night one man came alone to beat him, things changed.

The man was punching Jamil when his six-year-old son walked in, and before leaving, the attacker gave a fist blow to the boy's stomach that leveled him to the floor in pain. At that moment, Jamil's fatherly instinct kicked in, and after comforting his son, he grabbed a knife and went after the attacker. When he ran to the man's house, he told his elderly father that he was going to kill his son.

Notice the father's first response: "Jamil, this isn't like you."

No, it wasn't like him. But, as he told the father, he could take the beatings, but he couldn't handle the beating of his son. He had even threatened anyone who touched his son.

Guilt invaded that night, robbing Jamil of sleep. He had behaved just like them! Before sunrise he made his way to the home of the attacker to ask for forgiveness.

Yet the near-nightly beatings continued. Then one day, leaders of the local Islamist group barged in to attack Jamil before they left on a hunt. When they demanded that Jamil's wife cook for them, she complied. While she fixed dinner for them, Jamil talked to them about God. He even said, "May God bless your hunt." The men decided to forgo the beating that night.

Days later the leader asked for Jamil to come to his home to tell his family "what you shared with us the other night." A tormentor asking for truth from the one he tormented. Love opened the way.

Going Deeper

Jamil faced almost nightly physical beatings; you may face daily "beatings" of your own, whether verbal abuse or relentless stress. Only God's supernatural grace helped Jamil not to retaliate but to endure and forgive. Do you have situations in your life that tempt you to retaliate? God's same supernatural grace is available to you. Be grateful to use it, and then see what God will do.

Father, thank you for the faithful courage and endurance that Jamil showed to his tormentors day after day, year after year. We can't imagine enduring such abuse for so long, and we see sustaining strength in Jamil that only you can give. Continue to strengthen him and his family as they speak your truth and show your love to those who know only the language of violence. Use them in your supernatural way, and help us learn from their example. Amen.

Day 65

For the grace of God has appeared,
bringing salvation for all people.

Titus 2:11

At only seventeen years old, Hussein of Iran already held two titles that could have been his hashtags—#drugaddict and #drugdealer—titles that left him empty and searching one day while channel surfing, even though he couldn't identify his longing. But the man on TV spoke words that resonated with truth and hope.

And then the battle raged between Hussein's self-talk—*You're a drug dealer, a bad person, God hates you*—to God-talk: "God loves you, right where you are, whether you are a world ambassador or a drug addict … you matter to him."

Fortunately, God's truth won and Hussein committed his life to Christ. Everything changed. The appeal of drugs faded while his love for others grew. And then came the day his Muslim father reported him, in hopes that Hussein would be arrested. His father's anger was so great that he told Hussein he hoped he would be hanged as an apostate, adding that he wanted to be the one to put the rope around his neck. *His own father.*

The judge chose not to have Hussein executed, but he allowed the prison guards to perform their own justice. They broke one of his legs. They broke *all* of his fingers. Then before his release, they gave him forty lashes on his back. His high school expelled him and deleted all his records. Yet the words that came out of that refined-by-fire teen were these: "None of these punishments made me upset, except that I cannot play music for the Lord now."

Going Deeper

Like other Muslims-turned-Christians, Hussein couldn't help but talk about Jesus while he was incarcerated. The guard in charge of Hussein's torture was evidently touched, because he asked for Hussein to contact him. Why? Because he wanted to learn more. Think on this: when we talk about Jesus, there is always the possibility that someone will want to learn more. So why should we hesitate? With the freedoms we enjoy, let's share the life-changing truth about Jesus whenever we can.

Lord, we marvel at Hussein's amazing attitude, and we thank you for him and his heart for you. Thank you for the compassion you had on that teen boy who was watching television at a time ordained by you. We praise you for your orchestration and timing that only you can arrange. We pray never to deem something a coincidence but rather to see it as a means of grace. Help Hussein, and help us to walk in your Spirit and watch you at work.

We pray also for the ministry of Christian radio and television in countries that otherwise would hear little about you. Continue to expand those ministries, Lord, so that many more will hear truth and come to know you. Thank you for all the ways you make your name known. To you alone we give all the glory and praise. Amen.

Day 66

In the same way, let your light shine before others,
so that they may see your good works and give
glory to your Father who is in heaven.

Matthew 5:16

They live in a country where Christianity is legal, as it is here in America. People are free to switch religions if they like, just as we can here in America. Christians are permitted to build schools and hospitals that benefit their communities at large, just as we do here in America.

Yet on that January day in 2015, Christian men, women, and children of a village in the Zinder Province of Niger were running for their lives with gunshots ringing out all around them. Their thoughts raced as they ran, thoughts enveloped in shock and panic and fear. Why was this happening? Why were their own neighbors trying to kill them?

Pastor Mousa Tinibu was among those running, trying to reach safety. Stunned and overwhelmed by what was happening to him and his people, he knew they were experiencing for the first time the perils of persecution. The day before, protestors in French-speaking Niger demonstrated in response to the cartoon of a crying prophet Muhammad depicted on the cover of *Charlie Hebdo*, a French satirical magazine.

Now angry Muslims decided to target the small percentage of Christians living in their country, and they succeeded in killing 10 and leaving 170 injured. When the day of terror ended, the devastating losses included more than seventy churches, along with schools and orphanages, and more than a hundred houses belonging to pastors looted or destroyed.

How did the Christians respond to this evil? Like the body of Christ, they pulled together and helped one another. The Muslims in their neighborhoods noticed. And, as the body of Christ, they did the difficult thing and chose to forgive and love the Muslims rather than follow the downward path of revenge. One of the Muslims who noticed the contrast between the Muslims and Christians was a woman who accepted Christ as her Savior.

In the body of Christ, she saw the difference Jesus made.

Going Deeper

Did you put yourselves in their "running shoes" as the people of Niger were trying to escape for their lives? To hear that the country of Niger has enjoyed the same freedoms of faith as we do here in America chills us as we think about how quickly things can change. Pray that we prepare our hearts now both as individuals and as Christian communities so that we can emulate Pastor Mousa Tinibu's church in Niger.

Oh Father, how we pray to be the body of Christ in our neighborhoods and communities. Help us live and suffer and forgive in such a way that our every action and word point directly to you and to your love and forgiveness so freely offered on the cross. You suffered greatly for us, and may we never, ever take for granted your supreme sacrifice. Help us live in response to the

wondrous gift of grace you gave to us so that we can extend your invitation of grace to others.

Continue to use Pastor Mousa Tinibu and his people in the same way. Set them as a bright light on a hill—a shining example of your love so that all may see you and come to know you as Savior and Lord. Amen.

Day 67

Hear my prayer, O LORD;
let my cry come to you!
Do not hide your face from me
in the day of my distress!
Incline your ear to me;
answer me speedily in the day when I call!

Psalm 102:1–2

Put yourself in a city of half a million people. And then, as a believer in Jesus, think about being one of 0.7 percent of that population. That is the minority position of the 3,500 Christians who live in Gaza City. Now put yourself in the place of Rami Ayyad, who managed a Christian bookstore in that city dominated by Muslims.

The bookstore was bombed twice and threatened on a regular basis. But Rami remained. Why? In his words to his wife, "Jesus is the love of my life, and I will never deny him, regardless of what happens."

And something did happen. Three Muslim men kidnapped him, and the following morning his body was found near the store, riddled with bullet holes and knife wounds. He left behind his wife, Pauline, two children, and another child on the way.

Often, the ones left behind in the aftermath of a tragedy also become the victims of the violence leveled against their loved ones. When we put ourselves in Pauline's shoes, we can't help but feel her pain and anger—pain and anger that badgered her day after day and also blinded her. She hated Muslims. She hated everybody. She could see no good coming out of her husband's death, and she told God so.

Fortunately, Pauline still read God's Word in the midst of her dark valley, and the words of Ecclesiastes 3:2 gave her new understanding: "There is … a time to be born, and a time to die." God showed her that in his timing even the darkness of death is used for his plans. That verse set her feet on the path of forgiveness, but she knew her forgiveness of Rami's killers was at best superficial. The fullness of that forgiveness would take Pauline five more years on her faith journey.

Going Deeper

Anyone who has lived very long has experienced what has been called "the dark night of the soul," when the anguish of loss can overwhelm the strongest believer. A young mom's first experience of soul-shattering sorrow came when her almost full-term baby died at birth. Devastated by this unexpected loss, she tried to be "a good little Christian" to the outside world, only to go home and weep. She could hardly pray, but she often read the book of Psalms. One night the pent-up anger she had unknowingly suppressed for six months bubbled up until it came out in volcanic force, landing on page after page with her vehement words. And then she knew truth: God could handle her anger. He had been with her all along. It was then that her healing truly began.

What is our loving Lord speaking to you, his beloved child, right now? Be honest with him, and let go of whatever is holding you hostage and not allowing you to forgive and heal.

Lord, we can't imagine Pauline's pain as a young wife and mother, expecting her third child, when her husband and the father of her children was ripped away in what seemed to be a senseless tragedy. We thank you for Pauline's honesty and transparency as she struggled to cope with her husband's death—to forgive. Thank you for using your powerful Word to put her on the path to forgiveness. Thank you that you are not impatient with us but that you incline your ear toward us with loving compassion. Thank you for providing us with your strength when we fumble through the dark times that shroud our faith. Amen.

Day 68

Blessed be the God and Father of our Lord Jesus Christ,
the Father of mercies and God of all comfort, who
comforts us in all our affliction, so that we may be able
to comfort those who are in any affliction, with the
comfort with which we ourselves are comforted by God.

2 Corinthians 1:3–4

Just weeks after the funeral of a loved one, probably at least one person will offer the advice: "You need to get over it" or "It's time to move on." Usually those well-meaning people haven't dealt with a profound loss of their own, or perhaps they have done so by shoving down their own sorrow instead of dealing with it. Grief has its own timetable for everyone, and those who have experienced a deep loss come to realize that God will eventually lead them through the pain, not around or over it.

The Palestinian Bible Society moved Pauline and her family to Bethlehem, believing they would be safer there, but she still struggled to move on with her feelings of anger and animosity toward her husband's killers. Then five years after her husband's death, God broke through the shadows of her sorrow with the light of his truth: the Muslim men who killed her husband—and others like them—were the very ones she and other Christians needed to reach with God's love.

With that revelatory truth, Pauline was amazingly freed from the festering anger and bitterness, and everything became new: her spirit, her heart, her mind. She became full of forgiveness and acceptance, God's supernatural gift of healing.

Out of her healing came ministry to others. She reached out to Muslim women in her community by becoming involved in various outreaches. By opening a small gift shop at the Church of the Nativity, she began to provide for her family, with part of the inventory supplied by supportive Christians.

Now Pauline wears the mantle of a martyr's widow with honor and dignity. She has found in Jesus all that he promised to be: the husband, the father, the helper—everything. He is her reliable and dependable God.

Pauline's hard-won testimony now brings hope to other widows. She encourages them not to allow their husbands' deaths to become their own burial grounds. Instead, she offers the best counsel of all: "Experience Jesus and let him lift you up and use you in miraculous ways to bring glory and honor to his name."

Going Deeper

We won't ever "get over" a significant loss, nor should we; each one is a significant chapter that God can use not only in our lives but also in the lives of others.

God wastes nothing that happens to us. Every loss and sorrow lifted up to him—no matter how tragic, how painful, how beyond our understanding—he can use for his kingdom in ways beyond our wildest imaginings. Many ministries, large and small, have been born out of deep grief. Ask God if he has plans to intersect your pain with his plans to bring comfort and hope to others.

Our Lord, we praise you that you have transformed Pauline's painful journey into a journey of joy and purpose. Only you could do that, Jesus. Only you can take years of anger and bitterness and transform them into newness of life. We thank you for how you are using that newness of life in Pauline to bring healing and hope to others. Strengthen and encourage her as she helps other widows to truly know you in the fullness of who you are.

And help us allow you to heal any hurts in our lives, Lord, so that you can transform them into vessels for ministry. Wash from us any bitterness and resentment, and instill in us your newness of purpose. Like our sister Pauline, use us in the lives of others for their good and for your glory. Amen.

Day 69

*And falling to his knees he cried out with a loud
voice, "Lord, do not hold this sin against them."
And when he had said this, he fell asleep.*

Acts 7:60

Amina's baby was delivered stillborn. Doctors spent six
days suturing Amina's machete wounds and tending to a
fractured leg and gunshot wounds. She would spend many
months in the hospital. And all because of the Fulani assailants who entered her family's home on that April morning
in 2011. But it was the man with the machete raised above
his head whom Amina remembered the most, just before
he lowered it to slice her head, neck, and arms, leaving her
for dead.

Amina's husband was away on a hunt when the men attacked their village. When he visited her in the hospital, he saw the intensity of her pain from both physical wounds and heart wounds. She deeply mourned the loss of her baby and had wept for days after the attack. Her injuries made it difficult to speak, but when her husband asked her what she would do if she saw her attackers again, she looked at her injuries and, word by halting word, gave her answer: "Do to them … what they … did to … me."

A second question came from her husband. "You won't forgive them?"

Again the slow but deliberate words: "I will … never … forgive them."

Amina passed many weeks in the hospital, with lots of time to think and pray. When her husband returned, he asked the same question.

But this time Amina's answer was different. She told him that if she ever saw her attackers again, she had already forgiven them. The Lord had shown her that he had already known what was going to happen, and as Amina put it, "He has written it." Because she saw God's sovereignty, she went on to say, "Therefore, I will forgive them."

Eight months later she was stunned to see her assailant face-to-face when the man delivered firewood to her mother's home. They both recognized each other, and he couldn't look at her; he finished his business and left.

Later Amina said about all the attackers from that day, "I don't have any bad intention against them. Our prayer is that they would understand that what they are doing is not good so they will be saved when they die or when our Lord Jesus comes. Because if they died in this habit, they will not see God."

Going Deeper

Has someone wounded you? Have you forgiven that person? Your answer to this next question could be your indicator: Can you think now of that person without any animosity, with no negative feeling rising up within you? If not, consider writing a letter to pour out all your hurt and anger; paper is a safe place for a private release of woundedness. Then place those pages in your Bible and imagine God's Word absorbing the pain represented by every word while you immerse yourself in his Word at the same time.

Lord, to learn about the pain inflicted on this young mother wounds our hearts for her. Thank you for the work you did on her hurting heart while you were healing her body. How faithful you are to tend to our every need.

Give us hearts like Amina's, Lord—hearts that desire all people to be saved, from the hardened men who hurt Amina to the people in our lives who hurt us. Help us see beyond the exterior—beyond their deeds—to see the hearts of these hurting people who hurt others. We pray for Amina's assailants and all those who have turned to wicked ways to wound and kill others. Thank you that no one is beyond your grace and mercy. Help us never to forget that we are all sinners saved by grace and to remember to extend your grace and forgiveness to all. Amen.

Day 70

In the face of life's largest losses, forgiveness can take a long time. The devastation of horrendous happenings inflicted by the hands of others requires the supernatural grace of God to forgive. Amina found this to be true as she mourned the loss of her baby and recovered from all her wounds. Initially she said she could never forgive her violent assailants, but as time passed, God enabled her to do just that and to pray for their salvation.

A woman named Karen could relate to Amina's journey to forgiveness. Her abusive father always told her mother he would kill her if she divorced him. Her dad held positions in the local church but lived a different life at home. When her mother couldn't take the abuse anymore and obtained a divorce, Karen and her husband moved her mom to a secret place near them, taking every precaution to protect her.

Before Karen left to teach school every morning, she would call her mom to check on her. The day she didn't answer, Karen drove with dread to her mother's lovely mobile home. Inside she found her worst nightmare—her mom brutally murdered by knife wounds. Two young cousins had hidden in a closet in a back room, just as Amina's children had been hidden from her assailants.

Karen's anger burned within her toward the man she could no longer refer to as her "father"—and toward the divorce lawyer's secretary who exchanged her mom's address for a five thousand–dollar payment from Karen's dad. Tears flowed. Nightmares haunted her. But over time God did a mighty work of healing. Not only did Karen forgive her dad, but one day she went to the prison where he was assigned after the trial to tell him so. She left the prison freed from the shackles of an unforgiving heart.

Going Deeper

After Karen's mother was murdered, God led Karen to a career in counseling. Countless times clients have railed to her about people who have wronged them, always ending with, "I could never forgive them!" And countless times God has used Karen's own forgiveness journey to help her clients see that no one is beyond God's grace.

The path to forgiveness may be long, but it is well worth taking. Do you need to embark on that journey? God will be with you every step.

Dear Lord, what a difference you make in our lives! We know that true forgiveness comes only by your supernatural power and grace. Thank you that you love us so much that you give us the ability to forgive so that we won't have to bear the heavy burdens of resentment, bitterness, and anger.

Thank you for all the examples throughout history of Christians who have forgiven others of horrible acts against them. But we are acutely aware that it all began with you, Jesus. Hanging on the cross in agony, you spoke the words that echo with unending power and grace into eternity: "Father, forgive them, for they know not what they do" (Luke 23:34).

How can we do any less, Lord? How can we do any less than to forgive those who have wronged us, no matter how large or small the offense? Praise you, Jesus, for enabling us, by your Spirit, to forgive. Amen.

Day 71

*I appeal to you, brothers, by our Lord Jesus Christ
and by the love of the Spirit, to strive together with
me in your prayers to God on my behalf.*

Romans 15:30

A normal day. We have had many in our lifetimes without much thought—until an act of violence suddenly turns a day into anything but normal. Some folks enjoying their weekly Bible study at church. A police officer filling his patrol car with gas. Students going to class on their campus. People shopping at a mall. Folks enjoying a movie at their local theater. Nowhere in the world can any of us feel totally safe as the potential for evil acts exists everywhere.

We tend to associate acts of terrorism with the Middle East, but Muslim extremists are gaining a foothold in other countries as well. One of these places is Mindanao, the second-largest and southernmost island of the Philippines. Known for its mountain ranges, it is a popular destination for climbers, especially the country's highest peak, Mount Apo.

Mindanao has experienced ongoing violence between government forces and minority Muslim rebels. Muslim groups control four provinces on the island under the name of the Autonomous Region in Muslim Mindanao (ARMM). In October 2012 the government and the separatist Moro Islamic Liberation Front signed a tentative agreement to end the forty-year conflict, which claimed more than 120,000 lives in the island's southern region.

Most attacks against Christians occur in or near the ARMM, but incidents also occur outside the ARMM as terrorists seek to expand control. Muslim terrorists in the Mindanao region seek to force Christians out of their territory by taking land and livestock and killing Christians. They attack Christian villages in attempts to occupy the village or simply steal everything of value, leaving many widows and orphans in their wake.

A US official has dubbed Mindanao "the new mecca of terrorism," but the dedicated evangelical pastors and their people pray to see Mindanao called "a miracle of God's grace" instead.

Going Deeper

Spend some time getting acquainted with the areas of the world where our Christian family is suffering persecution. A great place to start is The Voice of the Martyrs website (www.persecution.com), where there are many resources to help keep you informed of current prayer needs. "Like" them on Facebook, and then be sure to check "get notifications." That way, when timely prayer is needed, you will be able to join a host of prayer warriors around the world praying for our persecuted fellow believers.

Father, we feel so ignorant not to have known what our brothers and sisters have been suffering around the world, including such places as the Philippines. Forgive us for being so centered on our lives that we have failed to look outside our circle of concerns. Although we have not intentionally meant to ignore them, we

thank you for how that has changed for us now. Thank you that our knowledge increases our prayers.

We pray for the Christians in Mindanao as they live life on the edge in so many regards. Protect them, Lord, from danger. Protect their hearts with your peace. Keep them strong in you. And we pray that you'll move the hearts of the Muslim attackers and bring them to yourself. Break forth with your truth and love, Jesus, and work a mighty miracle there. We pray in your powerful name. Amen.

Day 72

So now faith, hope, and love abide, these
three; but the greatest of these is love.

1 Corinthians 13:13

Do you tend to make a snap judgment the moment you see someone? Research has shown how we all do that very thing, whether we realize it or not; we determine our perceptions based on a person's clothing, hairstyle, ethnicity, age, or some other outward thing. We see the exterior and draw immediate conclusions, correct or not.

What if we put aside our biases and tried thinking a God-based thought for every person we saw? Here are three words to hang above the head of everyone you encounter: "*Longing for love.*" So, that rude person who cuts in front of you at the checkout line? "*Longing for love.*" The obnoxious loudmouth at some public event? "*Longing for love.*" The unfriendly neighbor? "*Longing for love.*"

That trio of words, "longing for love," came from Pastor Noel Vasquez, who lives in Mindanao, where our Christian brothers and sisters are suffering increased attacks from a minority of Muslims. In his words, "It's hard to win Muslims to Christ. But I love Muslims, because beyond the violence, they are *longing for love*. And I can share the love of Christ with them."

Pastor Vasquez is one of many Christians who have chosen to stay and not let hate win in the place he and his family call home. We can make the same choice. We can begin in the place we call home by looking at others with all the same need—*longing for love*—the love of Jesus.

Going Deeper

Whenever you are out and about, be mindful of those around you. Look at the downcast countenances. See the hopelessness in those empty eyes. Go beyond that prideful exterior and see past the facade. Envision a neon sign above each person's head or a large lanyard around each individual's neck that declares, "Longing for love." Or perhaps change the sign to "Seeking hope," or encompass their every wish with the sign we all can wear: "Needing Jesus."

Then be intentional about being Jesus to those around you as opportunities unfold. Offer a smile and greeting to the passerby while on your walk. Give words of encouragement to that overwhelmed store clerk. Allow the person behind you in line to go before you. Little things? Yes. But who knows in what big way God will use them? Especially when you also breathe a prayer for each person "longing for love."

God, thank you that your perspective always changes everything. Give us eyes of the heart, Lord—eyes that are so diffused with your love that we can look at others with only love. Fill us with your discernment to see the deep needs of others and with wisdom to best meet those needs, empowered by your amazing love.

Don't let us ever be put off by any exterior, Lord, but let us see each person with your eyes—the eyes of unconditional and unchanging love. We thank you for Pastor Vasquez and his heart for you, and we pray that you will protect and honor him and all the Christians in Mindanao who yearn to lead the Muslims there into a knowledge of your love. Amen.

Day 73

The steps of a man are established by the LORD,
when he delights in his way;
though he fall, he shall not be cast headlong,
for the LORD upholds his hand.

Psalm 37:23–24

When we read story after story of persecuted Christians, we see one thing over and over again—the ever-present hand of God. In the midst of each terrifying event is the undeniable truth of his presence and his provision. For those of us who are his, we can rest in the assurance of who he is—Emmanuel, *God with us.*

When Habila heard the pounding on the door that awakened him, his wife, and young son one warm night in Nigeria, he knew that God was with them. He was so stunned to see the masked and robed men, one with an AK-47, that words didn't come, but an inner prayer did: *Father, your will be done.*

Habila knew that God was with him when he did not hesitate with his answer to the question of whether he was a Christian or a Muslim: "I am a Christian."

He knew that God was with him amid their threats of death and his wife's tears, when he wouldn't profess to Islam, as they demanded, and instead remained silent. And when the gun was raised to his head, he knew that God was with him when he could tell his wife not to worry, because "the death of a Christian is a great gain, not a loss."

When he was left for dead after the bullet ripped through his mouth, Habila knew that God was with him as he whispered to his wife, "I ... am ... still ... alive."

Hours later, when medical help was finally reached, the doctor pronounced proof of God's provision: "It is only by God's grace that he survived." But God wasn't done intervening with his hand. The bone graft scheduled to repair his cheekbone had to be canceled, stunning the doctors. The cheekbone had healed, and the graft was no longer necessary.

Going Deeper

A beloved pastor once told his congregation, "Nothing will come to you that hasn't first passed before the eyes of Jesus … and he has given it his 'yes.'" Although some may recoil at those words, those of us who know and trust Jesus can take great comfort in them. We can initially see only the hardness of horrible situations, but God can see the broader picture, the entire landscape of his loving purposes. We may not see the situation from that vantage point until we view it from heaven, but we can be absolutely assured that God is working out his ultimate purposes for our good and his glory.

Pray for God to bring to mind past difficult circumstances, whether in your life or in the lives of others, and see how he will encourage you with the good he brought from those times for his glory.

Once again, Lord, we stand in awe and reverence of you, our amazing and almighty God. When we see your silent but powerful hand moving in the life of Habila, all we can do is

humbly praise you. Truly, there is no one like you, no god who can match your power, your grace, and your love. We praise you for your rescue and healing in Habila's life, and we pray that you will use his story in the lives of many.

Thank you, Jesus, for being our Emmanuel, God with us. Thank you that you are with us even when circumstances try to declare that you have deserted us. We cling with gratitude and trust to your promise that you will never leave or forsake us. Thank you that you and your Word are truth and totally trustworthy. We gladly and gratefully place our lives in your loving and caring hands forever. Amen.

Day 74

But thanks be to God, who in Christ always leads us in triumphal procession, and through us spreads the fragrance of the knowledge of him everywhere.

2 Corinthians 2:14

In our news-saturated world, little is left unknown these days. The stories that make the headlines often trumpet life's worst happenings, including trauma of every variety. *Post-traumatic stress disorder* (PTSD) is a term sadly familiar to all of us, in light of its many sufferers coming out of the conflicts in the Middle East. Trauma of all kinds can trigger the residual results of PTSD.

Habila, the Christian in Nigeria left for dead after being shot in his home, is a man of more than one miracle. His survival and the subsequent healing of his cheekbone without surgery were miracles gratefully received in the physical realm. But God also worked miracles in Habila's heart.

Ever since Habila returned home from the hospital and recovered from his wounds, he has been eager to share his story. His account of God's miraculous provision usually provokes the same question from his listeners. Most want to know Habila's feelings toward the masked men who tried to kill him on that night of terror in his home.

But Habila refuses to focus on the men. Instead, he brings his listeners into the conversation and focuses on the fact that we fellow Christians were all "condemned criminals" in need of God's forgiveness. He revels in the truth that Jesus loves us so much that he died for us. "That's why we must show love to the people who hate us."

Habila desires that the men who harmed him will come to know the same peace in Jesus that permeates his life. "I love them," he tells his listeners. "If I have the opportunity to see them, I will hug them and I will pray for them."

Only God could transform such intense trauma into triumph.

Going Deeper

If Habila's desire comes to pass, can you envision him hugging those men who so traumatized him and his family? What a beautiful picture of forgiveness and God's unfailing love!

With each retelling of his story, Habila is asked the same questions over and over. One of them is, "But how can you forgive the people who nearly killed you?" Can you hear the loving patience in Habila's voice as he answers? "Because Christ is love. The God I am serving is love. And he commands us to love one another."

Is there anyone—even an enemy—God has laid on your heart to love?

Lord, as we read Habila's words and hear his heart, we are transported to your heart of love for us. It is impossible to hear Habila's story without being moved and without seeing you at every turn. Thank you for your miracles of grace in his life. Thank you that you have transformed a devastating trauma in Habila's life into a striking triumph that he is using to proclaim

your truth. Thank you that, as in the story of Joseph, what was meant for evil you have meant for good.

We praise you for your amazing ways. And we pray for Habila, his wife, and his son, that you will continue to keep them in your care. We pray also for the men who came that night to do their destruction. Pursue them, Jesus, with your persistent love, and bring them to know you as their Savior. Amen.

Day 75

O death, where is your victory?
O death, where is your sting?

1 Corinthians 15:55

God's hope and victory are operative in Diya's life in Somalia, despite heartbreaking losses. The details of that day of devastation remain, even though God has brought healing. For more than twenty years prior, Diya had lived the life of a Muslim-turned-Christian, and he wasn't shy about it.

His most precious possession, a Bible in his own language, had survived a house fire that occurred at the beginning of the civil war in 1991. He loved reading the pages that were still readable, and that is what he had been doing that day when his six-year-old son, Amiir, picked it up after he set it down. When he was even younger, Amiir had followed in the footsteps of his father and mother and had invited Jesus into his life.

When he took his father's Bible outside moments later, the cross on the cover caught the eyes of two soldiers who were passing by in a vehicle. "Little boy, where did you get that book you are holding?" one asked. Amiir did not know that his truthful response would result in his and his mother's deaths that day. One bullet fired by one of the soldiers from a militant tribe killed both Diya's wife and son, leaving Diya with two remaining children.

The difference the Word made in Diya's life proved itself when, months after the attack, he spoke words of forgiveness toward the killer: "Loving and forgiving your enemies is good." Diya takes comfort in knowing that his wife and son are with Jesus Christ. He discovered the same truth as the one who taught his children that there are worse things than someone dying and going to heaven. Diya said, "There are other people who have been through worse treatment than me." And he is grateful that he is closer to Jesus than ever before.

Going Deeper

"There are a lot worse things in life than someone dying and going to heaven." That statement is palatable in light of life's brevity and the future hope of living with Jesus for all eternity. Our lives on earth represent only a small blip on the time line of eternity compared to the forever horizon of heaven. Savor each day as the gift from God that it is, share his love with others, but fix your gaze on the heavenly days still to come.

Father, all we can do is marvel at the amazing difference you make in the face of such tragedy. Your Word, your presence, your comfort are the elements that elevate painful loss to a lofty platform displaying your grace. It can't be explained or defined or denied, but it is real because of who you are. Continue to comfort Diya and use him and his testimony in the lives of many in Somalia and around the world. Amen.

Day 76

Create in me a clean heart, O God,
and renew a right spirit within me.

Psalm 51:10

His coworkers ran for cover at the sound of gunshots that November day in Nigeria, but Awuna ran for his motorbike. The threatening sounds of gunfire had started just after he began his shift as a hospital volunteer in the city of Jos. Aware of the children practicing at the church in his nearby village for an upcoming Sunday school program, Awuna feared for their safety. The nearly empty road only added to his alarm of seeing ominous smoke darkening the sky.

Screaming and shouting children at the church pointed to a can in the middle of the room—with a wire attached. *A bomb. The children!* Instinctively, Awuna grabbed the container to throw it out an open window. The explosion mangled his hands with shrapnel, and he saw the stunned and teary faces of the children above him just before he blacked out. But they were safe.

That act of selflessness set him on a difficult new path marked by months of indescribable pain, deep anger, and numerous surgeries to repair his horribly injured hands. For months he didn't even know where he was, or night from day, as he was enveloped in a fog that eventually dissipated. When it did, bitterness toward the bomb planters took its place, and a desire for vengeance surged against those who had hurt him.

Before that disastrous day, Awuna had succumbed to playing the role of a Sunday-only Christian. While he maintained worship attendance on Sunday, he mustered up only "shoulder shrugs" toward God the rest of the week.

No more. In the midst of Awuna's multilayered pain, God combined a collective force of fellow Christians who not only paid for Awuna's medical bills but also encouraged him with their visits, prayers, and reading of the Bible with him. The formerly dying embers of his faith ignited into a flaming passion. Those passing shoulder shrugs were transformed into a full embrace of God and his Word and a burning desire to share Christ with others.

Going Deeper

It took an explosion with severe pain and consequences to explode Awuna's faith from humdrum to exuberant. We refer to such a sudden catastrophic event in a person's life that shifts all of that person's parameters as a wake-up call. Awuna's thrust him into a deeper relationship with Jesus, and he is grateful. Consider whether you are in need of a wake-up call in your heart. If so, dig deep in God's Word, meet with strong believers, and pray for God's awakening in your soul.

Lord, thank you for Awuna, whose love for the children caused his reaction to protect them. We praise you for carrying him through all the painful months that followed. Thank you for all the Christians who rallied around Awuna with their loving care. We are so grateful for the difference they made in his life,

and we pray that you will bless them for blessing Awuna. Help us to be those followers of you who come alongside our fellow believers to bolster their faith in you.

Continue to use Awuna and his testimony in the lives of many. We pray that the story of his shattered hands will open many shuttered hearts to you, Jesus. Thank you again for yet another example of Romans 8:28 and how you work all things for the good of those who love you and are called according to your purpose. Amen.

Day 77

He said to him the third time, "Simon, son of John, do you love me?" Peter was grieved because he said to him the third time, "Do you love me?" and he said to him, "Lord, you know everything; you know that I love you." Jesus said to him, "Feed my sheep."

John 21:17

Have you ever wished for a second chance in a situation? A rewind on an episode in your life so you can replay it the right way—the way you wish you had the first time? Or maybe you would like to stand in the line of multiple second chances; it is likely many of us would join you there. After all, who hasn't experienced those times?

Awuna believes that God gave him a second chance that began the day he picked up that bomb to save the children. He had been sleepwalking through his journey with Jesus rather than being engaged as an enthusiastic traveler. But now all that has changed. His uplifting interactions with fellow believers and his commitment to Bible study, prayer, and fasting are key components in his faith walk.

Although Awuna was initially angry and bitter toward the men who caused such chaos and destruction that day, God moved his heart to the place of forgiveness. Awuna said that if he ever met the man who planted the bomb, he would tell him, "I forgive you for what you've done," citing how the Lord's Prayer instructs us to "forgive those who sin against us." After all, Awuna continued, "otherwise, our sins are not forgiven."

Awuna is grateful for every chance he has to tell his story to believers and nonbelievers alike. He is grateful that his heart is filled with forgiveness and that he is growing daily in Christ. He said, "God gave me a second chance to live in the world, and I want to live it for his glory."

Going Deeper

The desire for a "second chance at life" appeals to many, if the 133 million hits on Google give an accurate gauge. The scenarios of second chances for all of us would probably include these: taking back hurtful words spoken in haste, spending more time with that loved one who is no longer in our lives, standing for Jesus at a God-given moment rather than remaining silent.

Chance can also be defined as opportunity, and the good news is that we have a fresh opportunity in every moment that God gives us breath—opportunity to pray, to study God's Word, to encourage other Christians. Opportunity to shine Jesus in our corner of the world, to give light to the lost. Opportunity to say, "Thank you, Jesus, for being the God of countless chances to glorify you!"

Lord, we praise you for the many second chances you extend to us throughout our lives. We thank you that your mercies are new every morning and that great is your faithfulness to your

children. We praise you that the old passes away and that all things become new for those who come to you in faith. What amazing hope! What unbounded joy! What tremendous promises from you, our promise-keeping God!

Help us take advantage of every breath you give us so, like our brother Awuna, we can live this life for your glory alone. Amen.

Day 78

Therefore be imitators of God, as beloved children.
And walk in love, as Christ loved us and gave himself
up for us, a fragrant offering and sacrifice to God.

Ephesians 5:1–2

The story of the three men in Turkey whose throats were slit on what should have been a routine day at the office is beyond chilling. What they thought was a meeting to discuss faith with five young men turned into a torture session that terminated their lives. We can scarcely grasp what these Christians went through during such a sudden turn of events.

The three men made up the partnership for their business, Zirve Publishing House, a Christian publishing company. Tilman Geske, a German national and resident of Turkey for ten years, was working on a Bible translation. His partners, Necati Aydin and Unger Yuksel, were former Muslims who had converted to Christianity many years earlier.

In the midst of that grisly event, one thing we know for sure: Jesus was with those three men. He saw them and their suffering. He had not forgotten them. From the scene of those reprehensible actions, three martyrs were ushered into heaven and into the embrace of their Savior. God transported them from the gory of this earth into his glory in heaven in one swift moment.

But what about those who remained behind to deal with the aftermath of their deaths? What stunned the Turkish people then in 2007—and us today—is the grace-filled response of the wives: they forgave the killers. Immediately.

Susanne Geske's words bear hearing again and again as we think of those who have wronged us: "God, forgive them, for they know not what they do. I forgive the ones who did this."

Where does such grace come from? Susanne explains. "I had not had a single second of anger or anything in my heart—nothing." She related how the phrase "know not what they do" came to her mind. Her obvious heartfelt relationship with Jesus resonates with her words: "Because the Lord forgave me so much, so I have forgiven them."

Going Deeper

Amazingly, Susanne's daughters duplicated their mother's response to the murderers of their father. Again, this could be only God's doing. At first the older daughter was understandably angry, wanting to return to Germany, but months later she made known her desire to visit the assassins in prison so she could give them a Bible and pray with them. She wanted to share Jesus with them, and her younger sister concurred, expressing her hope for them to become believers. "And then if they die and come into heaven, they can tell Daddy and Necati and Unger that they are sorry."

"Amazing love! How can it be, that Thou, my God, shouldst die for me?" * God's amazing love births more amazing love—it is called forgiveness. Selah. Think on that.

---

*   Charles Wesley, "And Can It Be That I Should Gain?"
    www.hymnal.net/en/hymn/h/296.

Oh, dear Lord, once again we are reminded of your great love in such a poignant way. And we see like never before the gifts that come out of a love so matchless, so divine. Only you could give such a heart of forgiveness, such an attitude of acceptance that defies any human thinking, any human device. Only you, Lord. It always comes back to the magnificence and majesty of you. Praise you for imparting the gift of divine forgiveness. We worship you in reverence and awe, our amazing God. Amen.

Day 79

Every good gift and every perfect gift is from above,
coming down from the Father of lights with whom
there is no variation or shadow due to change.

James 1:17

When a woman was betrayed by the one nearest and dearest to her—her husband—she was devastated. Broken. Shattered. But in the midst of the shards of pain, God did an amazing thing, which she describes this way: "It was as if God lifted off the top of my head and poured in forgiveness—forgiveness that flowed down to my heart and then out to the heart of my husband. It was totally of God and not of me."

We have seen example after example of that kind of God-given forgiveness in these accounts of our brothers and sisters who experienced unbelievable pain and loss. Some arrived at forgiveness quickly—almost instantaneously—while others reached that point much later. God is kind and individual in his workings with his children. He, above all, knows us better than anyone and knows what each of us needs. While the time frames may vary, our Lord just wants us to move in the right direction—toward forgiveness and away from bitterness.

A willingness to forgive doesn't mean that the act of forgiveness removes the agony and ache of the loss. To love deeply means to grieve deeply. Necati Aydin's widow tells it as it is: "I suffer a lot. I'm going to suffer until the day I die."

Yet she gladly echoes the words of widow Susanne Geske when she says of her husband's assassins, "I didn't work to try to forgive them. God just gave me a gift."

Even in her grief and loss, this woman is thinking of others—those who have come to know the Lord because of her husband's death. "I know God showed his love to Turkey, not only on the cross but by Necati's blood."

Going Deeper

Have you thought about how forgiveness is a gift from God for us to give to others? Or did you think it was something you needed to work up on your own? Enter into the joy of accepting this gift from your Father and then gratefully pass it on to the one whom God is leading you to forgive. In giving forgiveness, you will receive the joy of obedience and the gifts of freedom and peace.

Lord Jesus, we lift up these dear family members of Tilman, Necati, and Unger. Only you truly know the depth of their sorrow and the consequences they have suffered because of the absence of these husbands and fathers. Comfort them, Lord, and give them your peace. May they be constantly aware of your everlasting arms around and beneath them.

Father, your Word tells us that every good and perfect gift comes from above, and we know that the gift of forgiveness is a direct gift from you, the Perfect One. Thank you for how you shine every time forgiveness is offered, and we give you the glory for doing in us what we cannot do on our own. Help us to be open to every gift from you, but especially help us never to forgo the vital gift of forgiving others. Thank you that in giving forgiveness, we gain freedom. We love you, Lord. Amen.

Day 80

I want you to know, brothers, that what has happened
to me has really served to advance the gospel, so that it
has become known throughout the whole imperial guard
and to all the rest that my imprisonment is for Christ.

Philippians 1:12–13

Even if you don't remember the name of Asia Bibi, most likely you will remember her story. Asia, a wife and mother, jailed in Pakistan on the charge of blasphemy, has made headlines around the world. Her case has drawn a bold line in the sand, with Christians petitioning for her release and other people calling for her death. Her death sentence, which has hung over her for years, was suspended in July 2015 by the Pakistani Supreme Court. Despite that, her future is still uncertain.

Asia's family was one of only three Christian families living in her village of fifteen hundred families. A farmworker, Asia spoke out for Jesus, declaring how he had died for her. She couldn't have dreamed of how her words spoken in a field would catapult her into the far-reaching realm of international news. The news has only escalated over the years.

Two officials in the Pakistani government stood up for her, one a Muslim and the other a Christian, and both were assassinated. Haunted by death threats, her family had to go into hiding and has moved several times since. A reward put out for her death has raised fears that Asia could be killed while in prison. In the meantime, her health has deteriorated during years of solitary confinement.

When first arrested, Asia was told she would be released if she converted to Islam. Her bold words revealed her brave heart: "You can kill me, but I will never leave Jesus." Her words also revealed what Jesus means to her and her love for him. How can she leave the one who loves her so much?

Going Deeper

Measure off an eight-by-ten-foot area in your home, and erect imaginary walls in your mind with no windows and a low ceiling. Furnish it with the bare minimum. No reading materials. No TV or electronic devices. Now imagine spending several years of your life only there, with no freedom to come and go. Imprint that image in your mind, or perhaps draw a diagram of it to use as a bookmark in your Bible, to remind you to pray for Asia and other Christians living in prison. Prayers for prisoners often bring their release, but our prayers can also bring relief and comfort while the bars remain. The longtime saying is true: "Prayer changes things."

Lord, our hearts ache at the difficulty of the daily consequences of Asia's stand for Christ. A husband and wife missing each other. A mother whose children are growing up without her. Bars preventing hugs from her family. We could go on and on. But we are greatly comforted to know that you are the Comforter and that you can make up for every gap, every need, in every life.

Your incomprehensible love cannot be contained or constrained in any way. You can choose an infinite number of ways to show your boundless care for your children. We pray that you will do that even now for Asia and her family. And we pray for other families who are suffering in various ways right now. Meet each need in your wisdom and perfect timing. We praise you for what you are going to do in each situation. Amen.

Day 81

Whom have I in heaven but you?
And there is nothing on earth that I desire besides you.
My flesh and my heart may fail,
but God is the strength of my heart and my portion forever.

Psalm 73:25–26

Have you been struck by how the members of our perse-cuted family are totally enamored with Jesus? He is truly their *all*—the whole of their lives, nothing but him, their *everything*. One little word, *all*, expresses a lack of nothing and the inclusion of everything.

In reading the stories of our family of God, have you pondered if you could respond in similar life-threatening situations with affirmations of faith? Our brothers and sisters would tell us, "Simply look to Jesus. He is truly all you need." When Jesus is our all, he will provide all we need. We don't need to project into the future or wonder if we are prepared. In the presence of Jesus will come what we need just when we need it, even as we live and face the pressures of life. The key is to live our lives now in the all of Jesus, and he will be *all* to us in whatever our future holds.

In Jesus, our all, comes the courage we need.

In Jesus, our all, overflows more joy than we can imagine.

In Jesus, our all, is strength for the fiercest opposition.

In Jesus, our all, is comfort for every sorrow.

In Jesus, our all, is contentment in every circumstance.

In Jesus, our all, is every need met that he deems needful.

In Jesus, our all, we can, with confidence, live and move and have our being.

In Jesus, our all, is the hope of this earth and the high hope of heaven.

Going Deeper

Sing or say the words to the chorus of this hymn written by James Rowe, and then write a prayer or psalm of praise to Jesus, your *all*.

All that I need He will always be,
All that I need till His face I see.
All that I need through eternity,
*Jesus is all I need.**

Jesus, our all, we could ask for no more than you. Help us see you as our all like never before. Nothing do we lack with you as our all. Nothing can be added to your completeness to make you more or greater. You are all. You are all-gracious, all-compassionate, all-loving, all-forgiving. In you as our all, we are complete. No straining, no reaching, no grasping—for anything. We have all that we need in you, and out of your fullness we pray that you will use us as we follow you. Thank you, dear Jesus, for being our all. Amen.

* James Rowe, "Jesus Is All I Need," www.hymnary.org.

Day 82

I have fought the good fight, I have finished the race, I have kept the faith. Henceforth there is laid up for me the crown of righteousness, which the Lord, the righteous judge, will award to me on that Day, and not only to me but also to all who have loved his appearing.

2 Timothy 4:7–8

These well-known words were penned by Charles Studd, often known as C. T. Studd:

Only one life, 'twill soon be past.
Only what's done for Christ will last.*

---

* All Studd quotations in this devotional are from Norman Grubb, *C. T. Studd: Cricketer and Pioneer* (Cambridge, UK: Lutterworth, 2014).

Charles was the youngest of six sons and was a famous English cricket player in the early 1880s. His brother George's serious illness confronted Charles with the brevity of life when in his twenties. He had come to faith several years earlier but confessed that the prior years had been spent in "an unhappy backslidden state."

He asked, "What is all the fame and flattery worth … when a man comes to face eternity?" As a result of his brother's brush with death, Charles concluded, "I knew that cricket would not last, and honour would not last, and nothing in this world would last, but it was worthwhile living for the world to come."

Studd left his world of comfort and fame to become a missionary to China, India, and Africa, and he was still laboring for the Lord in Iambi when he died at the age of seventy. He took joy in "living for the world to come" and influenced spiritual leaders who came after him.

Living for the world to come. We have seen that mindset in our persecuted brothers and sisters. Many have been stripped of everything material, but they cling to what matters: Jesus. Their joy is in their Lord. They are truly living for the world to come, with hearts to bring many with them into that heavenly kingdom.

Remember George, the brother of Charles who was extremely ill? The second born of the six brothers, he was one of the acclaimed English trio of Studd brothers who dominated cricket in the late nineteenth century. Instead of pursuing law, he too became a missionary. His mission field? America, where he lived and worked in a notorious and squalid area of Los Angeles from 1891 until his death in 1945. He evidently took to heart the words of his brother Charles, "Only what's done for Christ will last."

Going Deeper

God doesn't call all of us to the mission field, but he does call all of us to the joy of sharing the good news of Jesus with others. The third member of the famous Studd brothers cricketers was Sir John Edward Kynaston Studd, 1st Baronet, known as JEK or Kynaston. He led his life as a businessman and as the lord mayor of London in 1928. The speaker's remarks at his memorial service in 1944 reveal how God also used this Studd brother: "In his presence it was easier for men to be good and harder to be bad. Everything he touched he lifted up."[†]

Whose lives need to be lifted up to Jesus today? In what way can you touch them?

Dear Lord, we know the truth of the words "Only one life, 'twill soon be past. Only what's done for Christ will last," but we are so prone to forget with all the worries of this world and the countless distractions around us. Nevertheless, they are all unlasting, temporal, earthly things that will be left behind when we go to be with you, aren't they, Lord? Help us remember that we will go out of this world the same way we came in—with nothing.

And help us grasp and comprehend like never before the transforming truth that only the eternal will last—only the souls of people will live on. Peel back the lies of the enemy, and reveal to us your truth alone: to live is Christ and to die is gain. We pray that our every choice will be examined in light of eternity and that those choices will make a difference in the future roll call of heaven. Amen.

† The memorial speaker was F. H. Gillingham.

Day 83

So teach us to number our days
that we may get a heart of wisdom.

Psalm 90:12

What do you most enjoy doing? Although we have been focusing on doing those things with eternal value, we need to acknowledge that God provides a wealth of wonders in this world for our enjoyment, all out of his love for us. The Word tells us not to set our hopes "on the uncertainty of riches, but on God, who richly provides us with everything to enjoy" (1 Tim. 6:17).

Our friend from the past, C. T. Studd, the renowned cricket player, offers his perspective with these words: "I do not say, 'Don't play games or cricket' and so forth. By all means play and enjoy them, giving thanks to Jesus for them. Only take care that games do not become an idol to you as they did to me. What good will it do to anybody in the next world to have been the best player that ever has been? And then think of the difference between that and winning souls for Jesus."*

Now go back to that mental list of what you enjoy. Have you ever thanked Jesus for them, as C. T. Studd suggests? Or do you perhaps struggle with your pursuits of pleasure becoming your idols? The thing that you think about the most? The passion that consumes your time, maybe to the exclusion of what really matters?

Who doesn't grapple with those issues in our society, in which entertainment and leisure tend to be viewed as entitlements instead of an occasional privilege? If we were totally of the world, this discussion might even be ridiculed. But because we are believers in Christ, the answers don't come easily, nor is there "one size fits all." But it is something to pray about, isn't it? How we spend our free time matters when we think of all the lives that matter both near and far.

---

* Norman Grubb, *C. T. Studd: Cricketer and Pioneer* (Cambridge, UK: Lutterworth, 2014), 55.

Going Deeper

Social media has changed the landscape of our lives. On the plus side, it offers us God-given opportunities to pray for and encourage fellow believers, even ones we have never met. Yet is there anyone who hasn't experienced hours flying by when engaged online? As Christians and followers of God's Word, we desire to be mindful of the best use of our time and to lead Spirit-led lives. How does social media fit in to honor that mind-set?

The Internet is such an integral part of our lives that it is easy to forget how those minutes and hours could be spent on other endeavors, ones that would make a difference for eternity. Ask God if this is something he would have you do: estimate the minutes you spend each day on the Internet and match each one for equal moments of intercession for the worldwide church and other concerns. Even praying or interceding just once a week could have far-reaching implications for God's kingdom.

Lord, we are so thankful that you have told us we aren't to worry about anything but to pray about everything, even the seemingly small aspects of our lives. We can't help but recall that you have instructed us to walk wisely and to "redeem the time" (see Eph. 5:16) We do pray for your wisdom as we evaluate the use of our time and hold it up to the light of your Word.

We need your insight and guidance, Jesus. Help us to be so sensitive to your Spirit that every aspect of our lives will fall under your lordship. We never want an idol of any kind to usurp you on the throne of our hearts. Only a king belongs on a throne, Lord, and we pray that you, our Lord and King, will remain in that rightful position all of our days. Amen.

Day 84

There is no fear in love, but perfect love casts out fear.

1 John 4:18

Do you personally know any Muslims? Have you ever talked with them and gotten to know them? Have you invited them to your home? If you live in a rural setting with no Muslim residents, you may not have had an opportunity to meet any. But if you could, would you?

Tom and JoAnn Doyle, a missionary couple, have worked with Muslims for years, both in the Middle East and here in the States, and have observed that most Americans either hate them or fear them. Possibly both. Certainly the news coverage of the persecution and killings of Christians by Muslims has incited both emotions. But we can't justify either stance, because both are unbiblical.

According to Tom, Satan uses our fear and anger as a manipulative ploy to keep us away from Muslims. "After all, we have the truth and the light, so if Satan can keep us away from them, he's winning, right?" Yet the good news is that "in the last fifteen years, more Muslims have become Jesus followers than in fourteen centuries of Islam."

Tom and JoAnn admit that God had to break their hearts for Muslims because they weren't naturally drawn to them. Tom tells of seeing two men in a restaurant with "the look": black clothing, cropped beards. Tom thought they were terrorists, only to hear enough of their conversation to realize they were Christians.

We can learn much from Tom and JoAnn, as they urge us to pray for revival in our country. "Wouldn't it be cool if God reached a significant group of Muslims and they started evangelizing the Americans?" Tom and JoAnn's impassioned plea is "Use us here" and "May we rescue those who are perishing," including the 86 percent of Muslims, Buddhists, and Hindus who don't know one Christian. "Our hearts cry out for that to change."

Going Deeper

What would you think of someone who had the cure, the absolute cure-all, for cancer and yet refused to make it available to cancer patients? Hard to imagine, right? May that remind us not to be so cocooned and self-satisfied in our salvation that we forget how desperately others need Jesus. We have something far better than any cancer cure, because even cured people will eventually die. We have Jesus, the key to eternal life.

Consider adding a skeleton key or another unusual key to your key chain as a visual reminder of knowing Jesus, the key to eternal life. Maybe write a *J* on it. Who knows? It may turn out to be a conversation starter that could be the key to someone's salvation.

Dear Jesus, how can people know you if we don't show them your love? How can they know your salvation if we don't speak your truth? Break our hearts for the many who don't know you

so that your love can flow into our broken vessels and then into the hearts of others.

Help us to be your banner bearers of the gospel and replace our timidity with boldness. Remind us that this isn't about us and our hang-ups, Lord; this is about lost souls who are facing an eternity without you, and we long for them to know an eternity with you. Thank you for placing each of us in the corner of the world where you have chosen to use us. We humbly bow before you, dear Lord, until we hear your call for action and choose to respond in obedience. Amen.

Day 85

But when one turns to the Lord, the veil is removed. Now the Lord is the Spirit, and where the Spirit of the Lord is, there is freedom.

2 Corinthians 3:16–17

When you see a homeless person, do you avert your eyes and look the other way? How about when you see a veiled Muslim woman? Add to that list any others you are tempted to dismiss because of their differences. We have all been in that place of discomfort, haven't we?

JoAnn Doyle, a missionary to Muslim women in the Middle East and America, shares her heart for the more than eight hundred million women living under a veil. She wants us to be aware of the commonalities Muslim women share. "They learn at a young age they have no value; they have no voice." The women have been abused beyond what we can imagine, but they can't talk about it in a culture based on honor and shame.

The core of their problem is that very sense of no value; they feel "less than." The Quran gives husbands permission to beat their wives into submission. JoAnn emphasizes, "Muslims aren't the problem; Islam is the problem. Muslims are the victims." These women feel overlooked and forgotten.

If we look past them or look away, we are only reinforcing the lie that they are invisible, that they don't matter. JoAnn encourages American women to go past their preconceived ideas and move past their fears. Give eye contact and smile when you see a Muslim woman at the market or your children's school. Look beyond the veil and into her heart. Ask what country she is from, and ask about her children. Be genuinely interested and show the love of Jesus. The most important thing initially is to show Muslim women that you see them.

Be open and transparent about your own life and empathetic toward your new Muslim friends. If you have neighbors who are Muslims, take them cookies or brownies. As the friendships grow, ask how you can pray for them. When those bridges are built, the women can cross over into trust and will then share, often saying, "I've never told this to anyone in my life …"

Even if you never have the opportunity to share the gospel with a Muslim woman, you can be the one to plant the seed of God's love. We, as Christians, are the only ones with the message of hope. We can let these "forgotten women" know that Jesus hasn't forgotten them but loves and values them.

Going Deeper

Homeless folks and Muslim women aren't the only ones who feel invisible. A woman in her eighties told her family about how she feels invisible when she goes shopping. We have many opportunities to be the eyes of Jesus that truly see others, to let them know—even in small ways—that they aren't forgotten.

It is easy to get complacent in our comfort zone, isn't it? But think of what an adventure awaits when we instead become intentional about showing the love of our Lord. Follow his nudges and enjoy his outcomes.

Lord Jesus, we confess that too often we look the other way when our discomfort gets the better of us. Forgive us, Lord. Give us hearts like yours—hearts that see beyond appearances and into the hearts of others. Help us remember how alike we all are as ones made in your image. Help us break through false barriers so that we can benefit from the joy of fellowship.

You have given us the gift of eternal life, Jesus. Keep our fountain of life so overflowing that those who come into contact with us will want to drink of your everlasting life. We pray to see those around us like never before and to join in the opportunity to show your loving-kindness to this hurting world one soul at a time. Praise you, dear Jesus, for that precious privilege. Amen.

Day 86

Surely the righteous shall give thanks to your name;
the upright shall dwell in your presence.

Psalm 140:13

We have all seen images of Muslims bowing toward Mecca, their faces down to the ground five times a day. This ritual is one of many performed faithfully by millions of Muslims, often including the yearly pilgrimage to Mecca. And yet Islam is just that—a religion formed around rigorous rituals, always with the goal to do enough to reap their future reward. But when is enough *enough*?

No wonder so many Muslims are coming to faith in Jesus. The emptiness of their religion is being replaced with the fullness of a relationship with him. What they have sought after in all their *doing* they are now finding in their being with their Savior. They have tasted the dryness of religion, and now they are feasting on the richness found only in Jesus's presence.

Just as human relationships require time together to foster closeness, the same is true of our relationships with God. Snippets spoken in passing can't compare to time set apart for rich conversation. Intimacy grows and flourishes in times of heart-to-heart communion. It meets the deepest needs and longings of our souls. Nothing else can take its place. Basking in the presence of our Lord, simply enjoying him, is a treasure beyond measure.

The benefits of simply being with Jesus defy accurate description. When his presence is allowed to permeate every aspect of our lives, everything is brought to a new and meaningful level. No longer do we want to feast on the world when we can be nourished by manna from heaven.

This is what our persecuted brothers and sisters have discovered. Nothing is better than Jesus. No one satisfies like Jesus. Never could they consider denying the one whose loving presence in their lives has made all the difference.

Jesus is their first love, their true love, their supreme love. It is that love that settles every question and saturates them with peace. In light of life's most amazing love, why would we desire anything less?

Going Deeper

Although we may have added extra connotations to the word *grovel* over the years, its root comes from the Old Norse meaning "face down." The definitions expand on that term: "1. To humble oneself or act in an abject manner, as in great fear or utter servility. 2. To lie or crawl with the face downward and the body prostrate, especially in abject humility, fear, etc."*

See again the images of the face-down Muslims and compare groveling to *grace*: mercy, clemency, pardon, forgiveness, love. Then sing "Amazing Grace" with fresh gratitude and gusto.

---

* Dictionary.com, s.v. "grovel," http://dictionary.reference.com/browse /grovel?s=t.

Lord Jesus, we want only you. Forgive us if we have let you slip into the lesser priorities of our lives when what we really want and need is more of you. Restore to us the joy of our salvation. Give us a thirst and an appetite for you if those have dwindled or have even disappeared in our sated lives.

Our longing is for you, Lord—to know you, to really know you, so much so that we don't want to miss the sweetness of time in your presence. We don't want to miss what you might say to us, the comfort of your caring, the guidance you desire to give us.

But most of all, we want to enjoy your company, Lord—to tell you that we love you, to thank you for your sacrifice on the cross so that we can live with you forever, to praise you for your precious presence in our lives, which makes this life so worthwhile and gives us a foretaste of the one to come. Amen.

Day 87

If one member suffers, all suffer together; if one member is honored, all rejoice together.

1 Corinthians 12:26

The two questions asked of Muslims in Islamic nations before they become a Jesus follower are these: (1) Are you willing to be persecuted? and (2) Are you willing to die for Jesus? Can you imagine those questions being asked in membership classes in churches across America? As missionary Tom Doyle said, "In the Middle East, believers have to be ready to die for Christ. In America we're just looking for believers willing to live for Christ."

Although we in America would do just about anything to avoid persecution, and certainly we don't seek it, we do need to be aware of how God uses it. Persecution doesn't stymie the gospel; it grows it. When we look back through the history of Christendom, the times of great harvest in the church were always accompanied by persecution. Where is the church thriving and expanding most right now? In the lands and regions of the greatest persecution. God takes the pain of persecution and transforms it into glorious growth for his kingdom. The eternal far outweighs the temporal.

Consider this from Richard Wurmbrand, founder of The Voice of the Martyrs: "All of us have our burdens and sorrows. These are only shadows, because God, our Father, has another reality for us and sets for us an example of unspeakable love. Let us share that love with others, and let us bring to our suffering brethren a little joy."*

Going Deeper

We don't know personally the pain of persecution like our brothers and sisters are experiencing around the world, but as Richard Wurmbrand beautifully states, "Christians should know what is happening to their brothers and sisters all over

---

* Richard Wurmbrand, "Suffer with Patience and Quietness," *The Voice of the Martyrs*, February 2001, 10–11.

the world.… We must preach Christ and Him crucified, but what about my brothers and sisters? They are so valuable that Christ died for them; therefore, Christ Himself wishes that we know what happens to them. We should love them. We should shed a tear of compassion for them. We should help, in a small measure in which we can, those who are never too far away for love."[†]

What small measure can you take today?

Our Father, thank you that no one is ever "too far away for love" because of your all-encompassing love. The persecution we have read about and have even seen on screens in our homes hasn't been a part of our personal lives, but because it is happening to our family of faith, it is happening to us, for your Word teaches us that when one part of the body suffers, we all suffer.

Thank you for the fellowship of your family all around the world. Thank you that we can lift one another up in prayer and together experience the sweetness of your Spirit always with

[†]   Richard Wurmbrand, "How Are Your Brothers?," *The Voice of the Martyrs*, March 2001, 12–13.

us. What a wonderful, limitless God we serve who can be in abundant measure in every believer throughout the world, with nothing lacking. In you, Lord, is all-sufficiency for all things for all time and beyond. Praise you!

With that truth in mind, we lift up our suffering brothers and sisters in Christ and ask that you meet with them in the abundance of your Spirit and give to each one what is needed at this very moment. Help us all to keep our eyes on you, Jesus, until together we gaze on your face and lift our hearts of praise in one heavenly hosanna. Praise you! Amen.

Day 88

And I heard a loud voice from the throne saying, "Behold, the dwelling place of God is with man. He will dwell with them, and they will be his people, and God himself will be with them as their God. He will wipe away every tear from their eyes, and death shall be no more, neither shall there be mourning, nor crying, nor pain anymore, for the former things have passed away."

Revelation 21:3–4

Do you find it challenging to read the painful stories of our persecuted brothers and sisters in Christ? That is such an understandable response. We wish we could file these accounts under fictional horror stories, but instead we face the fact that they are real. And we need to know that realness for the sake of those suffering.

These worldwide family members of ours don't want to be put on a pedestal or be pitied. But they do desire our prayers. They need to know they have our support. They need the sense of that sweet fellowship in the Spirit despite the oceans and deserts between us.

These fellow believers are like us, with the same faith in the same Lord. They just happen to live in places where that faith often requires sacrifices unfamiliar to us in America. We and our brothers and sisters are traversing everything from jungle paths to freeway jungles, but the path of our hearts is headed in the same direction—to be faithful followers of our Lord Jesus Christ, to know him intimately, and to live as lights aflame for him and his kingdom.

We are in this together. Although differences abound, our oneness in Christ is what defines us, what gives us determination to stand together for him, what reminds us that we are not of this world but of the one to come where one day we will all be united in our heavenly home.

Think on that: *our heavenly home.* Can you imagine the sounds, the sights, the colors, the utter joy and love—*divine* love and joy without a single sin stain or mar of any kind? And the best part? To be with our Jesus forever. That is our future; that is our hope; that is what makes every hard thing here worthwhile. This isn't the end of the road; this is our jump-off point to heaven.

When we live in that reality, when it grabs us at the core of our being, then there is nothing better than being a part of this phenomenal family of faith, both here on earth and in the heavenly realm beyond. That reality is so worth living for—and dying for.

Going Deeper

Quietly meditate on what awaits us in heaven. Search out scriptures on that topic, and then, whether it is Christmastime or not, sing all the verses of "O Come, All Ye Faithful"* and adore our Lord with fresh gratitude. "For he alone is worthy, Christ, the Lord."

Praise you, Jesus, for those times when you give us a glimpse of our future with you in heaven. Thank you for our astounding

---

* John Francis Wade, "O Come, All Ye Faithful," www.hymnary.org.

family of faith around the world and for all the generations that have gone before us. How we anticipate with great joy and expectation the heavenly reunion awaiting us—a reunion to outdo every reunion here on earth combined, hands down! We can't help but smile and well up with excitement when we embrace the incomparable truth of that future reality.

Keep that vision of victory before us, Lord. More than anything, keep your face before us, dear Jesus, so that we can even now look at you in wonder and praise.

"O come, let us adore him! O come, let us adore him!" Amen.

Day 89

But you are a chosen race, a royal priesthood, a holy
nation, a people for his own possession, that you
may proclaim the excellencies of him who called
you out of darkness into his marvelous light.

1 Peter 2:9

In these pages we have learned more about our family
around the world, our brothers and sisters in Christ. With
more knowledge and insight, we know better how to hold
them up with our prayers. But just as we know others better
after being in their homes, we can feel even more connected
to our worldwide family when we visit where they live.
Because we can't travel to every country, the Internet and
books can help take us to the homes of our brothers and
sisters in Christ.

Can you point out the country of Niger on an un-labeled map of Africa? How about Nigeria? Most of us could probably stand to brush up on our geography to see exactly where these newfound friends of ours live. Watch videos taken in their countries. Enjoy getting better acquainted with the countries these family members of ours call home.

Find out what languages they speak and what foods they eat. Explore the natural habitats and see the plants that grow there and the animals that dwell there. You can even see what time it is there and what kind of weather they are enjoying. Look also at photos of the landscapes and of their residences, the places they call *home*.

When we immerse ourselves in the diverse cultures, hear the languages they speak, and see the landscapes of their lives, we can pray with more connection and fervency for our fellow believers.

Going Deeper

You may be fully informed on the nations of the world, but often our daily schedules and cares keep us from learning as much as we'd like. To simplify, "adopt" a country, learn all you can about it, and then focus your prayers there until God moves you to another one. Don't worry if none of that is possible. The main thing is this: *pray.*

Dear Lord, what an honor and joy and privilege it is to pray for those we have never met. Yet we are related; we are family! Thank you for our brothers and sisters from every corner of the world and how one day there will be no boundaries, no oceans, nothing to separate us from each other in the home you have prepared for us.

Thank you for the richness found in each culture and all that we can learn about each other and from each other. But, above all, thank you for the same hearts that beat within all of us—hearts for you, Lord, filled with worship and praise. What a celebration awaits us. Praise you! Amen.

Day 90

To the King of the ages, immortal, invisible, the only
God, be honor and glory forever and ever. Amen.

1 Timothy 1:17

Different countries
Different cultures
Different climates
One body in Christ.

Different languages
Different livelihoods
Different lifestyles
One body in Christ.

Different colors
Different clothing
Different customs
One body in Christ.

One in our love for our Lord
One in our desire to serve him
One in our passion to reach others
One body in Christ around the world.

Together we pray in unity
Together we stand in faith
Together we join in love
One body in Christ around the world.

Someday we'll be together
Someday in heaven we'll sing
Someday we'll shout the victory
"Jesus! Our Lord and King!"*

* Poem written by Judy Gordon Morrow, author of *The Listening Heart*.

Going Deeper

Close your eyes and envision the reality of heaven. Especially think about all the believers who have gone on before us, from those of biblical times to modern-day martyrs to your dear friends and loved ones. What a glorious reunion that will be—a celebration of our Savior that will last forever. *Forever.* An eternity of pure joy. Place that perspective against any persecution here, and know the glorious truth of the beloved song "When We See Christ" by Esther Kerr Rusthoi:

> *It will be worth it all when we see Jesus!*
> *Life's trials will seem so small when we see Christ;*
> *One glimpse of his dear face, all sorrow will erase.*
> *So bravely run the race till we see Christ.*[†]

---

†   Esther Kerr Rusthoi, "When We See Christ," New Spring, 1941, www.hymnary.org.

Jesus, our Lord and King, we can hardly wait to be united with all our brothers and sisters from around the world and throughout the ages to raise our praise to you! Thank you for the oneness, the fellowship, the love that we know from being a part of the body of Christ. There is nothing more sublime this side of heaven, and we will continue to praise you here until that day when we will praise you there with hearts overflowing with love. Amen.

Are You an "N" Christian?

To learn more about your persecuted family members and to get your church involved, go to *www.i-am-n.com/products*.